STAR Performance

Uniting Planning and Doing for a High Performance Leadership Model

Justin Thompson, PhD

What People Are Saying about STAR Performance

The book's concepts are critical to the success of our actions and in particular to our actions in business. Oftentimes, business leaders gain the understanding of these concepts much later in their careers and based on too many avoidable mistakes along the road ... The outstanding feature of the book is that it draws the interactive lines between planning and execution in a logical, concise, and understandable manner ... This book will be a valuable tool in setting a meaningful course for your business, implementing such course, and ensuring that you stay on course over time.

—Paul Wolmarans, CEO, Kenpat

Justin Thompson's *STAR Performance* is poignant and powerful, helping individuals and teams move toward excellence! Use his system, and you will find yourself reaching for the stars!
—Dr. Joel Breidenbaugh, Senior Pastor, First Baptist Sweetwater

STAR Performance is very well put together. I like the conciseness and practicality of the material. The presentation is very clear and engaging. It's well worth the time to read and will be a helpful reference tool for productivity in the future as well!

—Doug Gordon, CEO, Newsome Oil

It is worth exploring this work with patience and seeing it through to the finale ... I feel it is a high-level work for upper-level managers, or executives, who are looking to improve their headset and strategies ...
—Robert Scaglione, Hanshi, Ju-Dan, CEO, Shorin-Ryu Karate USA

Excellent concepts with good analogies and explanation. A must-read for any executive.

—Brian Cummings, President, BCA Technologies

Copyright © 2015 Justin Thompson, PhD

All rights reserved. No part of this book may be used or reproduced by any means, graphic, electronic, or mechanical, including photocopying, recording, taping or by any information storage retrieval system without the written permission of the author except in the case of brief quotations embodied in critical articles and reviews.

Scripture quotations are from The Holy Bible, English Standard Version® (ESV®), copyright © 2001 by Crossway, a publishing ministry of Good News Publishers. Used by permission. All rights reserved.

Scripture taken from the Holy Bible, NEW INTERNATIONAL VERSION®. Copyright © 1973, 1978, 1984, 2011 by Biblica, Inc. All rights reserved worldwide. Used by permission. NEW INTERNATIONAL VERSION® and NIV® are registered trademarks of Biblica, Inc. Use of either trademark for the offering of goods or services requires the prior written consent of Biblica US, Inc.

WestBow Press books may be ordered through booksellers or by contacting:

WestBow Press
A Division of Thomas Nelson & Zondervan
1663 Liberty Drive
Bloomington, IN 47403
www.westbowpress.com
1 (866) 928-1240

Because of the dynamic nature of the Internet, any web addresses or links contained in this book may have changed since publication and may no longer be valid. The views expressed in this work are solely those of the author and do not necessarily reflect the views of the publisher, and the publisher hereby disclaims any responsibility for them.

ISBN: 978-1-5127-1683-2 (sc)
ISBN: 978-1-5127-1684-9 (hc)
ISBN: 978-1-5127-1682-5 (e)

Library of Congress Control Number: 2015917250

Print information available on the last page.

WestBow Press rev. date: 11/20/2015

Contents

Preface ix

STAR Importance 1
    STAR 3
    Planning (Strategy and Tactics) 3
    Doing (Action and Results) 4
    Facing Our Giants 5
    Review 8

Strategy 11
    Purpose 11
    Principle 13
    Passion 15
    Application 21
    Review 30

Tactics 35
    Preparation 37
    Planning 39
    Prioritization 44
    Application 50
    Review 55

Action 57
    Practice 58
    Persistence 62
    Perspiration 66

Application	68
Review	70

Results 73

Patience	74
Productivity	77
Probing	78
Application	83
Review	84

Performance 87

Precepts	88
Attitudes	98
Review	113

Appendix—Worksheets 119

Preface

Thank you for picking up a copy of *STAR Performance*. I hope that you will not only read these pages but also absorb and apply the content. My goal in writing this book is to help you discover new truths and new perspectives so that you find yourself energized and excited about the direction in which you are headed. When you apply the high performance leadership model that you will learn in this book, you and your team will be invigorated by a harmonious sense of purpose, imaginative direction, and a passion-inspiring vision that transforms you and your organization into thriving success machines.

You will gain an awareness of your failures and challenges as the stepping-stones to success that are necessary to achieve the abundance of limitless possibilities existing before you. If you're going to flourish, you first have to learn to fly, and sometimes that requires falling out of the nest a few times before you take flight and soar to new heights of performance.

Each chapter of this book discusses a particular portion of the STAR Performance model. Whenever possible and appropriate, I've sprinkled in some colorful stories, examples, and graphics to help illustrate the concepts and make them more engaging and memorable. Additionally, at the end of each chapter, you will find a list of review questions. To get the most out of the time that you invested in reading this text, I suggest writing down your answers to these questions. You may also find it helpful to use these as discussion starters when studying through the concept with your team or other group. Such group discussions are ideal ways to sharpen the concepts and use them as building blocks to construct something new and exciting.

The appendix portion of this book contains a number of worksheets that can be used in your planning exercises. You may go through these yourself or contact me at the e-mail address provided below to inquire about executive coaching services to help guide you and your team through the process.

I wish you the best of success in all that you endeavor to accomplish, and I eagerly await your comments, questions, and feedback.

Best regards,
Justin Thompson
Justin@2Xalt.com

Chapter 1

STAR Importance

> "Cheshire-Puss," she began rather timidly ... "Would you tell me, please, which way I ought to go from here?"
> "That depends a good deal on where you want to get to," said the Cat.
> "I don't much care where—" said Alice.
> "Then it doesn't much matter which way you go," said the Cat.[1]

The cat was on to something. If we have no sense of purpose, objective, or plan of any kind, then it really doesn't matter what we are doing. We might feel good about ourselves for staying busy and having lots of "work" to do, but are we really accomplishing much? If we are lucky—blindly lucky—we might actually accomplish something with all our busyness. When we have the clarity of a plan that provides purpose and direction, a target to aim for, and an objective to strive toward, we will accomplish so much more.

Plans are important to success, but our efforts cannot end with a plan. There has to be action—real, tangible, mud-on-your-hands action. Just as it is true that action without plans may lead us in the wrong direction or simply be inefficient, it's also true that planning without action is just a waste of time. In most cases, the planning portion of our efforts should be relatively small in comparison to the action—an ounce of planning for pounds and pounds of action. All too often, we jump into the pounds of action before taking time for the ounce of planning. The result is typically in line with the proverb about struggling to the top of the ladder only to realize the ladder is leaning on the wrong wall.

> When we have the clarity of a plan that provides purpose and direction, a target to aim for, and an objective to strive toward, we will accomplish so much more.

If we start construction of a major skyscraper without any blueprints or engineering analysis, we aren't likely to have a successful project when all is said and done. Blueprints are the tactical plans for building projects. Even before the blueprints are drawn up, the architect needs to know what we want to accomplish and why the building needs to be designed. Otherwise, we may end up with a perfect design for an office building when what we really need is a museum. On the same note, though, if we design the most impressive blueprints and construction plans but never break ground, erect steel, or build anything, what was the point?

Thomas Edison said, "Being busy does not always mean real work. The object of all work is production or accomplishment and to either of these ends there must be forethought, system, planning, intelligence, and honest purpose, as well as perspiration."[2] He understood that thought had to be given to why effort was being made and what one hoped to accomplish by doing the work. At the same time, he also understood that having such a plan is not the end of the project; it is the beginning. He knew one had to put much effort into taking action—perspiration—if success was to be achieved.

STAR

The point of this book is to draw the lines of connection between the planning and the doing. STAR is an acronym for strategy, tactics, action, and results. We must weave these components together in such a fashion as to achieve tangible performance improvements. Planning involves defining the strategy and tactics that will be used going forward. The doing involves getting your hands dirty in diligent action and the close look at the results of that action.

When each of these components—strategy, tactics, action, and results—is illustrated as an arrow, we want to see those arrows all pointing at the same target. If they point in random directions, we end up with nothing but a bunch of arrows leading us nowhere. When they all point at the same target, as illustrated at the beginning of this chapter, the STAR becomes apparent.

Planning (Strategy and Tactics)

Our performances can only be optimized or improved when we carefully and intentionally march through each step in this process in order of priority. Setting a strategy must always come first. This is because our strategy defines both *what* we are going to do and *why* we going to do it. It also defines the principles by which we will govern our actions and those of our organizations.

A tactical plan that carefully defines how we will work toward the strategic plan is also part of the planning process. As a matter of fact, tactical planning should be the bulk of the planning process because it defines the operations or programs that will let us fulfill our strategies. It is the final component of planning before we step out and take action, and it is critical when we desire to raise a team of people working toward the same objective. It determines what tactics will be used to achieve success and what programs and projects will be pursued to bring about that vision defined in the strategy. Without a tactical plan, our team may work extremely hard, but everyone isn't necessarily rowing in the same direction. At best, we'll struggle heavily to stay on course, but most likely, we'll just be going in circles.

Doing (Action and Results)

Some get caught up in the planning and never start doing. This is a critical mistake. Planning is essential, but I would liberally apply the eighty/twenty rule such that we spend 20 percent of our time planning and 80 percent doing. This ratio is not set in stone, of course. It is merely meant to emphasize that we do not want to overlook the planning, but we don't want to overemphasize it either. Once a plan has been developed, we want to focus our attention on getting it done. This doing should consume most of our time and efforts.

Once action has begun, we must diligently monitor and measure results so that we can make adjustments to the plan along the way. Some components of our plans should be rigid (core purpose and values), but most of it must maintain some level of flexibility. In life, things change. We must be able to adapt and overcome if we are to avoid extinction. This may mean abandoning a plan, or a significant portion of a plan, but usually it just means making course corrections to the plan.

For example, we may have a mission to break into a particular market and a set of major projects designed to help us succeed in doing so. As time goes on, we may find that market conditions have changed such that one of those projects no longer has the potential that it once had (or that we once thought it had). We may be tempted to keep at it because we've already put in so much effort. But if succeeding at the project will do nothing toward achieving our original objective, we either need to change the objective or drop the project.

Facing Our Giants

Have you heard the ancient Hebrew story of David and Goliath? Goliath was a giant warrior who taunted the Hebrew army and blasphemed the Hebrew God. David was a young shepherd boy visiting his brothers, who were soldiers in the Hebrew army. David had predefined components of his "strategy" for purpose and values. He was sure his purpose in life was to honor his God, and his values were built around that purpose. When he witnessed Goliath's taunting and blasphemy, David didn't question for a second that he now had a clear mission to accomplish—end the taunting and blasphemy of the giant. He exhibited flexibility in his planning by adapting to the changing environment around him, but he never wavered from his core purpose or principles.

Once he accepted this new mission, others tried to do David's tactical planning for him. The leaders didn't delegate it to the one with the mission as they should have. They tried to equip him with armor and weapons that he had no experience with; David would surely have been killed had he carried them into battle. As leaders, aren't we sometimes guilty of doing the same thing? Rather than defining a vision for our teams and then coaching and encouraging them as they develop the tactics to be used to

STAR Performance

achieve this vision, we often micromanage and try to define the tactics for them. This may work at times, but we usually end up arming people with weapons they can't use or are just not right for the battle in front of them.

David developed his own tactical plan. He would charge the giant armed with a sling and five stones. This wasn't a rash and impulsive decision. He had years of experience with his weapon of choice, having previously defended his flock from a bear and a lion by using only his sling and bare hands. He knew exactly what he was doing. His plan was simple. It was executable. It was well within his level of expertise. And because David had a strong foundation of core purpose and principles, this tactical plan only took seconds to develop.

He even developed contingency plans. Some may think he carried five stones in case he missed the first time, but the truth is he only had time for one shot. If he missed, Goliath would have been on top of him like the fierce warrior that he was. The other four stones weren't backup ammunition for Goliath. They were meant for the four relatives of Goliath that were likely standing in the background, or any of the other warriors with him.* David

---

* Goliath is described as a giant from Gath, an Anakite. There are four other giants that are described as descendants of the Philistine giant in Gath in 2 Samuel 21 and 1 Chronicles 20. They are "Ishbi-benob, one of the descendants of the giants"(2 Samuel 21:16), "Sippai, who was one of the descendants of the giants (1 Chronicles 20:4) ... Lahmi the brother of Goliath" (1 Chronicles 20:5), and an unnamed "man of great stature, who had six fingers on each hand and six toes on each foot" (1 Chronicles 20:6). Some speculate that the "giant(s)" that these are descended from could be referring to Goliath himself (so that the four other giants would be three sons and one brother to Goliath) or to an ancestor that was also a giant (making the relatives a brother and three cousins). The Bible, our only significant historical record of this event, does not clearly state that these four relatives of Goliath were present when David killed Goliath; however, it is certainly possible, and even likely, that they would have been present as they were part of the Philistine elite fighting force, along with Goliath. I believe David

was ready for the battle to grow bigger than it originally appeared. He had a contingency plan!

David's plan succeeded. He slayed the giant and didn't need to use his contingency. You will face giants in your life and in the life of the teams, or organizations, you lead. Have your strategy (purpose, values, and vision) predetermined so that when new missions present themselves, you can quickly develop a tactical plan and then jump right into execution. In this way, you will slay your giants and come out on top!

---

collected the four extra stones to prepare for additional attacks that might occur after his confrontation with Goliath, whether those attacks might have come from Goliath's giant relatives or others in the Philistine army.

STAR Performance

Review

1. What does the acronym STAR represent?

2. What are the two key components of planning?

3. What are the two key components of doing?

4. When all of the elements of STAR are aimed at the same target, what happens to our performance?

5. What is a good rule of thumb measure for the split of our time between planning and doing?

6. What "giants" do you currently face in your life or the life of your organization?

Notes

[1] Carroll, Lewis. *Alice's Adventures in Wonderland*. Illust. John Tenniel. MacMillan and Co., London, 1866, 89. Web. June 16, 2015.
[2] "Work." *Wikiquote*. Web. June 8, 2015. Thomas Edison, as quoted in *Ford Times*, vol. 6, 1912, 136.

Chapter 2

Strategy

Purpose | Principles | Passion

Strategic planning is really about defining why we exist, what we endeavor to accomplish, and what guidelines we will adhere to in the process. It is simply developing a core plan that provides a sense of *passion* inspiring *purpose* and is guided by a set of nonnegotiable core *principles*. I call this the three Ps of strategy: purpose, principles, and passion.

Purpose

At the most fundamental, core level, the why component of strategy should be constant—unchanging over time. It is a definition of our core purpose—the meaning of life or existence, if you will. While our understanding of purpose may deepen or evolve over time, our core purpose is set in stone. Changing it will fundamentally change the organization (or individual) to which this purpose is referring.

When preparing himself for painting the now famous masterpiece *The Last Supper*, Leonardo da Vinci wrote this statement within his notes: "Make your work in keeping with your purpose and design."[1] Purpose is something we define initially and don't need to redefine every time we make new plans. Instead, our purpose should be intricately woven into our vision, missions, tactical planning, and action. All future activity should reflect this purpose. Da Vinci didn't just pick up a paintbrush and wait for inspiration to strike. He planned, prepared, and set out a course of action with intent and conviction. Then, after all the planning and preparing was complete, he took brush in hand with the knowledge that his work would reflect his "purpose and design."

> While our understanding of purpose may deepen or evolve over time, our core purpose is set in stone. Changing it will fundamentally change the organization (or individual) to which this purpose is referring.

To understand our core purpose, we simply keep asking "Why?" until we get to the foundation. Why are we doing this? Why is that important? Why do we need this? Why are we striving to make a profit? Why? Why? Why? Eventually, we will settle on our fundamental, core purpose and thus identify why we exist. In this way, we "draw out" the purpose that is in our heart. There is an ancient Hebrew proverb that illustrates this process. "The purpose in a man's heart is like deep water, but a man of understanding will draw it out."[2] If we want to be people of understanding, we must learn how to "draw out" our fundamental, core purpose—our reason for existing.

This purpose is different from mission. The two are often confused and the terminology interchanged, but purpose is fundamental and foundational, while mission is environmental. Our purpose is a definition of <u>why</u>, while our mission will define <u>what</u> we are going to do in the here and now to fulfill that purpose. They are different, yet both are very important components of the strategic planning process. Missions will change and adapt over time, and we are likely to find that we have multiple missions at any one point in time. Purpose, however, is unchanging.

Purpose should be the very first thing we define in our planning process. It should come before any other planning, and certainly before action is taken. If you run full steam ahead without a clear purpose, you are likely to run in circles or find you made a lot of progress in the wrong direction. When working with teams, you simply cannot expect your team to be effectively headed in the same direction if they don't have a clearly defined, common purpose. Your team won't get passionate about what they are doing if they don't know why they are doing it. On the other hand, if they have a strong sense of why they are working on a particular mission, and they really believe in the cause, then nothing will be able to stop them from succeeding! By the way, if they don't believe in the cause (purpose), then you don't want them on your team anyway. And how will you know if they believe in the cause if you don't communicate this cause to the team?

Principle

Defining a purpose also requires adopting principles, or values, that the organization will adhere to. This is critical! As individuals, we must define and adopt such principles well before we are in the midst of the proverbial battle. If we do not, then our principles will be shifty and shaky—tempted to alter in the face of challenges.

It is not the purpose of this text to define your principles for you but to emphasize the importance of defining your principles up front. Having said that, I would propose that amongst the most important principles, or values, we could adopt for ourselves, and for our organizations, are honesty, integrity, and courage. Honesty is critical, because if people can't trust what you say, they will eventually find someone that they do trust. Integrity is closely related to honesty—it is living out your principles in your day-to-day actions. It is a life that reflects the character of honesty in daily action. Courage is important, because there will come a time when a courageous heart and strong backbone will be required to maintain your principles of honesty and integrity. Courage is also required to take the risks that are essential for growth and long-term success.

For instance, if we have honesty as a strongly defined and adopted principle, then when the temptation to lie to a customer in order to close a major sale comes along, we will be willing to give up the sale rather than violate our honesty principle. If this is a clearly defined principle of the organization, then your team will know the boundaries and understand the expectations to be honest, even when it hurts to do so. On the other hand, if we just give lip service to honesty without strictly adopting it as a nonnegotiable principle by which our organization will govern its actions, then we, or our salespeople, will "bend the truth" (lie) in order to make that sale.

Which company would you prefer to do business with? Which company is most likely to get repeat business? Remember that if honesty is not expected between your team and your clients, then your team members will not default to being honest with you either.

Whatever you desire for your principles to be, whatever you desire for people to think of you and your organization, must be clearly defined, continually communicated, and exceptionally maintained as a standard for the organization. If this is not the case, then the principles you desire may not actually be the principles that your organization lives by, or is known for.

Strategy

As an example, I want my organization, 2Xalt, Inc., to be known as trustworthy, with a strong sense of optimism, a high degree of excitement for the value of the work that we are doing, and tremendously courageous. These principles are built upon HOPE, as demonstrated by the acronym defined below.

Honesty — A central core of integrity that shows through in everything that we do. Simply trustworthy character.

Optimism — An eternally optimistic perspective that sees potential around every obstacle and seeks the good in all situations.

Passion — An excitement for what we do and zeal for the success of those we serve.

Energetic courage — A sense of bravery in the face of challenges that is filled with energy and excitement, driven by passion for the cause.

Passion

Passion is what we want to create from our planning. We want to be passionate about the vision for the future and the things we endeavor to accomplish. We will have a mission, or series of missions, which we will need to get our team passionate about. How do we generate this passion in ourselves, and in our team?

> This harmonious combination of inspiring purpose and meaningful vision is what generates passion.

It starts with the purpose, as previously noted. When we have an exciting purpose, it is much easier to generate passion. Even so, there has to be more to it than a strong, exciting sense of purpose. There must be a meaningful vision attached to that purpose that points in a direction that you, and your team, are genuinely excited about and energized to fulfill. This harmonious combination of inspiring purpose and meaningful vision is what generates passion.

Vision

Vision is strategic intent. It is simply a picture of what the future will look like (or how you want the future to look). It is a dream that has been fashioned and molded into an image that can be communicated to others. A wise man once said, "Vision is the art of seeing what is invisible to others."[3] This is very true. It is an art, and it is all about seeing something beyond the ordinary. It is about seeing potential that others overlook. And it is about communicating this potential in a way that inspires others to get passionate about it as well.

Every leader must develop a vision that gets people excited. Great leaders encourage others to develop visions of their own. As the art of visioning spreads, the vision for your organization and all that can be accomplished will grow and grow. It will be your job to keep all of this visioning on target—aimed directly at the core purpose. This is true whether you are a CEO setting the corporate vision, a department head setting a vision for your department that is complementary to the corporate vision, or an individual employee developing a personal vision and striving to get those around you on board.

> Once you've inspired people to passionately follow your vision, and develop complementary visions of their own, you've created real, unquenchable passion that is a fuel for action that simply cannot be beat.

Once you've inspired people to passionately follow your vision, and develop complementary visions of their own, you've created real, unquenchable passion that is a fuel for action that simply cannot be beat. Steve Jobs famously put it this way: "If you're working on something exciting that you really care about, you don't have to be pushed. The vision pulls you."[4] This is exactly what I'm talking about. Get excited about your vision. Help your team become passionate about the vision. Then you won't have to expend any effort on motivation because the vision will pull you, and your team, along.

There are those who believe they must "crack the whip" over their teams in order to get things done, and I will admit that there is a time and place for such urgent pushing. If my house is on fire, I don't want the responding firemen to take time to inspire me to be passionate about their job. Crack the whip over me to get me out the window as quickly as possible! I don't want them to be concerned with my long-term loyalty to their cause. But a true leader knows that long-term success of the team requires loyalty, passion, and excitement.

Think about recent history. When the US military invaded Iraq with the intent of overthrowing Saddam Hussein, many of the Iraqi troops simply surrendered when the US troops approached them. There was a lot of fighting, for sure, "but often, the opponent advanced with a white flag in hand, instead of a rifle."[5] Some of them even surrendered to journalists. It might be said that this is because they felt the overwhelming superiority of the US military, but I don't think this is true. History is full of examples of militaries and militia that were cornered and overwhelmed but didn't give up because they believed their cause was too great—worthy of any sacrifice required of them. (Think of the American Revolution, the Alamo, the storming of the beaches of Normandy …) These Iraqi troops simply didn't believe in the cause that they were enlisted to fight for. The heavy-handed forceful tactics used to obtain their services worked as long as there were no other options, but as soon as another viable option presented itself and tested their loyalty to the cause, they abandoned their mission and surrendered.

If you use heavy-handed, forceful tactics to motivate your team, you'll win their immediate action, but you won't win their hearts. You'll generate action in the short term, and you'll find your greatest talent working for your competitors as soon as the opportunity presents itself to your team. Instead, you must inspire passion and loyalty. To do this, you should communicate your vision with a statement of colorful imagery that summarizes it in a memorable way. The wording should be such that it inspires and can be easily memorized and personalized by everyone on your team. Your vision needs to be communicated in such a way that you do not need to "push" your team. Instead, their common acceptance and passion for the vision will pull them on its own.

Mission and Objectives

To be able to clearly articulate and communicate a vision, you will need a succinct list of key desired outcomes that define accomplishment of the vision. These key desired outcomes, or targets, are strategic objectives. An objective is simply that which you are seeking to accomplish. The terms *goals* and *objectives* are often used interchangeably, so at this point, I would like to clarify the distinction between the two terms, as I use them. When I talk about objectives, I'm speaking of strategy. When I speak of goals, I'm referring to tactics.

Mission and objectives are always linked as strategic components of vision. Goals and programs or operations are always linked as tactical components of the plan. In other words, objectives are associated with the "big picture," while goals are associated with the shorter term. This is not a universally accepted, written-in-stone distinction that is true everywhere these two terms are used, so always pay attention to what is being said in order to really understand what is meant. In this book, the term *objective* will always be strategic and linked with mission, while the term *goal* will always be tactical and linked to an operation or a program.

Strategy

We'll address goals more in the chapter on tactics; here, we will address the strategic missions and objectives.

Objectives are measurable and definitive strategic targets. Objectives and mission are parallel, rather than serial, components to a passion inspiring vision. This means they are interrelated and feed from one another. You may have a single mission and multiple objectives, multiple missions and a single objective, or multiple missions and multiple objectives. The point is you must have both mission and objective to articulate vision.

A mission is a strategic assignment delegated to, and accepted by, an individual or team. If a team does not accept a mission, or is not passionate about the completion of a mission, successful accomplishment of the mission is unlikely. The acceptance of, and dedication to, the mission is critical. This is driven by the passion invoked within the team. A purpose that they believe in, principles that they are proud of, and a vision that inspires them are essential ingredients.

Your organization may have a singular mission, or there may be multiple missions. Whether you have just one mission or a dozen, every mission that you have must be supportive of the core purpose already defined.

Your purpose defines why you exist. Your principles define how you will govern your actions. Your passion defines a vision that inspires, objectives that clarify, and missions that give direction.

Your purpose defines why you exist. Your principles define how you will govern your actions. Your passion defines a vision that inspires, objective(s) that clarify, and mission(s) that give direction. The objectives provide *scalar* quantities. This means they communicate only a magnitude (e.g., the desired outcome). Mission provides a direction—a heading for your travels, like a compass. Passion is a *vector* quantity—where an inspiring vision is communicated with objectives that provide a magnitude and missions that provide trajectory (direction).* As previously noted, missions and objectives are parallel components to vision.

Missions may then be applied on one or more mission fields with one or more programs or operations. The missions are strategic—aimed at fulfilling the vision in light of the core purpose. The programs and operations are tactical endeavors meant to fulfill the mission in support of the strategic plan.

As an example of this strategic planning process, consider the US involvement in World War II. The purpose of US involvement was essentially the restoration of peace to the world. General Dwight Eisenhower gave an "Order of the Day" to the troops about to participate in D-day. Although this address was specifically for one operation within the WWII strategy, excerpts from it provide a very good glimpse of the vision that inspired a nation to action and the world to have hope. He stated,

> The eyes of the world are upon you. The hopes and prayers of liberty-loving people everywhere march with you ... you will bring about ... security for ourselves in a free world.
> Your task will not be an easy one. Your enemy is well trained, well equipped and battle-hardened. He will fight savagely ...

---

* Within the world of mechanics, there are two fundamental types of quantities: scalar and vector. A scalar quantity is a quantity of magnitude alone. For example "I'm traveling at fifty-five miles per hour" is quantity of speed—telling you how fast you are moving but giving no indication of direction. Therefore, speed is a scalar quantity. However, if you stated "I'm traveling due north at fifty-five miles per hour," you've communicated the quantity of velocity—a vector quantity providing both magnitude (fifty-five miles per hour) and direction (due north). For our analogy, to get passion, you need both the objective (the magnitude of the vision) and mission (the direction for how to fulfill the vision).

I have full confidence in your courage, devotion to duty and skill in battle. We will accept nothing less than full Victory!

Good Luck! And let us all beseech the blessing of Almighty God upon this great and noble undertaking.⁶*

This is a vision that inspires passion, loyalty, and commitment. It inspired thousands of men to charge into battle knowing that, despite their fears, they were fighting for a worthy cause. They believed, and rightfully so, that the freedom of peace-loving people throughout the world was in their hands. Many of them paid the ultimate price of sacrificing their lives for that vision. And they succeeded! We owe our freedom today to these men and their unfailing commitment to the vision of freedom, and the overpowering of fascism. This is why they are known as "the Greatest Generation."†

The objectives of US involvement were discussed and debated at the Trident Conference attended by President Roosevelt and Prime Minister Churchill. Churchill proposed to FDR and the Joint Chiefs that the objectives be

1. to "get Italy out of the war by whatever means might be best";
2. reducing the strength of the German offensive on the Russian front, or, as Churchill put it, "taking of the weight of Russia";

---

* I've included excerpts that are directly applicable to the larger vision of the entire US involvement in WWII. The full statement includes much more detail regarding specifics to Operation Overlord—the D-Day assault—a tactical operation in support of the strategic mission to restore democracy, and more specifically the strategic objective of liberating Western Europe from the Nazis.

† I would quickly point out that we have a generation of men and women alive today that exhibit many of the same traits of self-sacrifice and passion for societal good that was so keenly demonstrated by "The Greatest Generation."

3. to "apply to the greatest possible extent our vast Armies, Air Forces, and munitions to the enemy";

4. liberating Western Europe with a "full-scale invasion of the Continent from the United Kingdom as soon as possible"; and

5. providing aid to China and developing a long-term plan for the defeat of Japan.[7]

Notice the terminology used in these objectives: "whatever means might be best," "taking of the weight," "the greatest possible extent," and "full scale invasion." These were not "give it our best shot" kind of objectives. These were all-or-nothing, do-or-die, totally focused efforts to overwhelm and annihilate the enemies of freedom and democracy—because to fail meant the destruction of liberty, a failure that was simply not acceptable. The entire free world knew these objectives, and every man, woman, and child in this free world was passionately motivated to see them through.

Multiple tactical operations were carried out in support of each of these strategic objectives. For instance, Operations Husky, Baytown, Avalanche, and Slapstick were all part of the objective in the Mediterranean to end Italy's involvement in the war.[8, 9] Operations Bolero, Pointblank, and Overload were major portions of the efforts to fulfill the objective to liberate Western Europe. Bolero was the buildup of US troops in the United Kingdom.[10] Pointblank was the air strike and bombing initiative designed to destroy German industrial capability and air superiority.[11] Overload was the ground assault, ultimately known as D-day, which carried enormous cost yet successfully achieved the objective and overpowered the Nazis.[12] These are all tactical operations meant to achieve the strategic objectives. In some cases, one operation may be all that was needed for an objective, and in most cases, each objective required multiple operations to be successfully reached.

Strategy

WWII Strategy

Purpose: Peace on earth

Vision: Security for ourselves in a free world

Mission: Restore democracy by winning the war against fascism and tyranny.

Objectives:[*]   [1] Remove Italy from the war.

[2] Weaken German presence on Russian front.

[3] Build strength and might of attack.

[4] Liberate Western Europe from Nazis.

[5] Liberate Asia from Japanese forces.

The point is that there must be a core purpose that gives our teams and organizations meaning. There must be principles that put the entire team on the same playing field with the same rules of conduct. And there must be passion that comes from an inspiring vision, clear objectives, and a set of missions that provide direction. This is strategy. The components working together like gears in a transmission box.

---

[*] You might just as easily define a mission for each of the objectives, rather than a single mission defined by the multiple objectives. To some extent, how this is actually articulated is left to personal preference. I tend to give preference to simplicity. Thus, when it makes good sense to do so, I prefer a single mission with multiple objectives. If you told me you preferred a separate mission for each objective, I would not declare that you were wrong but would likely suggest a simplification in messaging might make communication of the plan more easily accomplished.

| 23 |

Initiatives

One final component of passion is a listing of strategic initiatives. These initiatives are strategic plans that define a means or method for bringing the vision into reality. They may be short-term, very specific strategic projects to move the organization closer to the vision, or ongoing elements of the overall strategic plan that enable day-to-day progress. Short-term initiatives include, but are not necessarily limited to, major reorganization or reengineering efforts, major system changes to bring business systems in better alignment with the vision, or culture change efforts designed to guide your team to passionately back the vision. Ongoing initiatives may include elements of a strategic plan, or business model, such as market strategy, value strategy, channel strategy, or operational strategy.

Application

We now understand that a strategic plan—that is the strategy for moving forward—is the foundational component to the planning process. It consists of three major components—the three Ps of strategy.

| Purpose | Principles | Passion |

Purpose is our most fundamental reason for being. It is why we exist. It is at our very core—the center of who we are as an individual or as an organization.

Principles are the guiding values by which we govern our actions. These principles may be built upon greed and selfishness, or they may be built upon honor and integrity. The choice is entirely yours, yet you must make a choice. You have the freedom to define your principles and how you will govern your actions, and the decisions that you make will determine how you are known and respected over time.

Strategy

Passion is generated by a sense of a cause worth fighting for. It comes from developing a vision that inspires you and your team, and the defining of objectives and missions in support of that vision. To communicate your vision, you will want to develop an inspiring and memorable vision statement with clearly defined strategic objectives. Once this vision is defined, your team will develop a series of missions in support of the vision (or a singular mission focused on the vision). The leader will be tasked with helping the team narrow the focus to the most critical of the missions, building the team as needed in support of these missions, and acting as coach to encourage, motivate, and inspire the team(s) working on the mission(s).

This strategic plan doesn't have to be overly complicated or drawn out. But it does need to be clear, effective, and inspiring. You need to lay this groundwork before developing the plans for specific actions, to ensure that you and your team are focused on the right actions, guided by commonly accepted principles, and targeting the same objectives. The development of purpose and principles should be fairly straightforward—just putting into words what you already know. The development of specific strategic objectives may be a little more involved.

In the end of this strategic planning, we want to create an awareness of direction, build clarity of purpose, and inspire limitless passion for the cause that ultimately yields thriving results and successful endeavors.

As you start to really think through this, you may find that clarifying these objectives not only helps you communicate with your team but also helps you focus your own thoughts and efforts on the objectives that you really want to accomplish. Oftentimes, what we initially think should be our objectives is actually different from what we settle on for objectives after carefully thinking through this strategy. In the end of this strategic planning, we want to create an awareness of direction, build clarity of purpose, and inspire limitless passion for the cause that ultimately yields thriving results and successful endeavors.

	Strategy
Purpose	Why: The fundamental reason for existence.
Principle	Values: The guiding nonnegotiable tenants that govern behavior.
Passion	Vision: Strategic Intent; An inspiring, prophetic insight to the future.
	Mission: Strategic Assignment; The specific duty charged to the organization in support of the core purpose
	Objectives: Strategic Targets; Outcomes that give measurable clarity to vision.
	Initiatives: Strategic Plans; Plans that define a means or method for bringing a vision into reality

There are many examples of good strategic plans the clearly articulate purpose, principle, and passion. At that heart of these plans are simple, short, articulate, and inspiring statements of vision. Ford Motor Company declares, "Ford today is driven by three priorities: accelerating the pace of progress on our One Ford plan; delivering product excellence with passion; and driving innovation in every part of our business."[13] Google declares, "Google's mission is to organize the world's information and make it universally accessible and useful."[14] Microsoft's vision is to "empower every person and every organization on the planet to achieve more," and they go on to describe "bold ambitions" (objectives) as [1] "reinvent productivity and business processes," [2] "build the intelligent cloud platform," and [3] "create more personal computing."[15]

Strategy

One of my favorite examples comes from PepsiCo. It is one of my favorites simply because of how it is organized and communicated. The plan is outlined on the following pages:

PepsiCo Purpose ("Our Commitment")

"To deliver SUSTAINED GROWTH through EMPOWERED PEOPLE acting with RESPONSIBILITY and building TRUST."[16]

PepsiCo Principles

They list five simple principles.[17]

1. Care for customers, consumers, and the world we live in.
2. Sell only products we can be proud of.
3. Speak with truth and candor.
4. Balance short term and long term.
5. Win with diversity and inclusion. Respect others and succeed together.

PepsiCo Passion

Recall that passion is built on an inspiring vision containing both mission and objective. PepsiCo describes a series of objectives that are communicated as fitting into one of four categories: performance, human sustainability, environmental sustainability, and talent sustainability. I love this categorization, because it clearly communicates the connection between the objectives and the mission.

If I had to critique the plan, it would be for their choice of terminology. They call the mission a goal, but it is clearly a mission. If it were a goal, it would consist of clearly measurable metrics. They define these clearly in the objectives, which is exactly where they should be in a strategic plan. Despite this semantics variation, I think the PepsiCo plan is articulate and well thought out, and it

STAR Performance

will be a good example to touch upon throughout this book. I've summarized the PepsiCo vision, mission, and objectives below.

Vision   Performance with purpose[18]

Mission   Deliver top-tier financial performance while creating sustainable value for all stakeholders.[19]

Objectives[20]

1. Performance: Strive to deliver superior long-term financial performance and sustained shareholder value.
2. Human sustainability: Continue to refine our food and beverage choices to meet changing consumer needs by reducing sodium, added sugars, and saturated fats, and developing a broader portfolio of product choices.
    a. average saturated fats per serving reduction of 15 percent by 2020
    b. added sugar per serving reduction of 25 percent by 2020
    c. average sodium per serving reduction of 25 percent by 2020
4. Human sustainability: Continue to provide clear nutrition information on our products and sell and market them appropriately to our consumers, including children, in line with our global policies and accepted global standards.
5. Environmental sustainability: Help protect and conserve global water supplies, especially in water-stressed areas, and provide access to safe water.
6. Environmental sustainability: Innovate our packaging to make it increasingly sustainable, minimizing our impact on the environment.
7. Environmental sustainability: Work to eliminate solid waste to landfills from our production facilities.

8. Environmental sustainability: Work to achieve an absolute reduction in greenhouse gas (GHG) emissions across our global businesses.
9. Environmental sustainability: Continue to support sustainable agriculture by expanding best practices with our growers and suppliers.
10. Talent sustainability: Create a safe, healthy, diverse, and inclusive workplace that reflects the global communities in which we operate.
11. Talent sustainability: Respect human rights in the workplace and across the supply chain.

STAR Performance

Review

1. What are the three Ps of strategy?

2. What is the difference between purpose and mission?

3. What is the very first thing we should define in our planning process?

4. How would you define purpose for yourself? For your organization? (See worksheet 1 in the appendix.)

5. What are principles, and why is it important to define them up front?

6. What would you define as principles for yourself? For your organization? If they are different in any way, why? (See worksheet 2 in the appendix.)

7. What generates passion?

8. What is "vision"?

Strategy

9. Fill in the blanks. Your _____ defines why you exist. Your _____ defines how you will govern your actions. Your passion defines a _____ that inspires, objectives that clarify, and missions that give direction.

10. What are the three main ingredients to passion?

11. What is a mission, and what does it provide?

12. What is an objective, and what does it provide?

13. What is the difference between goals and objectives? Which are strategic, and which are tactical?

14. Where are missions applied?

15. What is your mission—for yourself and for your organization? (See worksheet 3 in the appendix.)

16. What are your objectives for yourself, and for your organization? (See worksheet 4 in the appendix.)

17. Write your vision statement, summarizing your mission and objectives with colorful imagery that paints a captivating picture of the desired future. (Do this from both the perspective of your personal life vision and the vision for your organization.) (See worksheet 5 in the appendix.)

Notes

1. Williams, Jay. *Leonardo Da Vinci*. New Word City. 2014. According to Mr. Williams, this quote is an excerpt from Da Vinci's notes in preparation for painting his now famous *The Last Supper*. Emphasizing the importance of planning even further, Mr. Williams writes, "After much thought and study, Leonardo began the painting."
2. "Proverbs 19:21." Holy Bible: English Standard Version. Crossway Bibles, 2001.
3. Swift, Jonathan. *Values.com*. "Foundation for a Better Life." Web. April 9, 2014.
4. Jobs, Steve. *Values.com*. "Foundation for a Better Life." Web. April 9, 2014.
5. Hancock, David. "Iraqis Surrendering in Hordes." *CBS News*. Web. March 21, 2003. <http://www.cbsnews.com/news/iraqis-surrendering-in-hordes/>.
6. "Order of the Day." *Dwight D. Eisenhower Presidential Library, Museum and Boyhood Home*. National Archives and Records Administration. June 6, 1944. Web. March 9, 2015.
7. "Trident Conference." *Dwight D. Eisenhower Presidential Library, Museum and Boyhood Home*. National Archives and Records Administration. June 6, 1944. Web. March 9, 2015.
8. Hickman, Kennedy. "Invasion of Italy, 1943—World War II." *About Education: Military History*. About.com. Web. March 9, 2015. <http://militaryhistory.about.com/od/WWIIEurope/p/World-War-Ii-Invasion-Of-Italy.htm>.
9. "Allied Invasion of Italy." *Wikipedia*. Wikimedia Foundation. Web. March 9, 2015.
10. "Chapter IX: Case History: Drafting the BOLERO Plan." History.army.mil. US Army. Web. March 9, 2015. <http://www.history.army.mil/books/wwii/WCP/ChapterIX.htm>.
11. Emerson, William. "Operation POINTBLANK: A Tale of Bombers and Fighters." USAF Harmon Memorial Lectures. USAF. Web. March 9, 2015.
12. "World War II: D-Day, the Invasion of Normandy." *Dwight D. Eisenhower Presidential Library, Museum and Boyhood Home*. National Archives and Records Administration. Web. March 9, 2015. <http://eisenhower.archives.gov/research/online_documents/d_day.html>.
13. Fields, Mark. "Letter from Our President and CEO." *Ford Motor Company 2014 Annual Report*. 2014. Web. July 24, 2015. < http://corporate.ford.com/annual-reports/annual-report-2014>.

[14] "Company Overview." *Company—Google*. Google. Web. July 24, 2015.
[15] Nadella, Satya. "Satya Nadella E-mail to Employees on Aligning Engineering to Strategy." *Microsoft News Center*. Microsoft. June 17, 2015. Web. July 24, 2015.
[16] "PepsiCo Values." *PepsiCo Performance with Purpose: Sustainability Report 2013*. PepsiCo. Web. July 24, 2015, 66.
[17] "PepsiCo Values." *PepsiCo Performance with Purpose: Sustainability Report 2013*. PepsiCo. Web. July 24, 2015, 66.
[18] "PepsiCo Values." *PepsiCo Performance with Purpose: Sustainability Report 2013*. PepsiCo. Web. July 24, 2015, 1.
[19] "PepsiCo Values." *PepsiCo Performance with Purpose: Sustainability Report 2013*. PepsiCo. Web. July 24, 2015, 1.
[20] "PepsiCo Values." *PepsiCo Performance with Purpose: Sustainability Report 2013*. PepsiCo. Web. July 24, 2015, 9.

Chapter 3

Tactics

Preparation | Planning | Prioritization

Tactics are the methods, procedures, and plans to be used to achieve the desired result (e.g., the objective). Strategy defines what and why, and tactics define how. In other words, the mission and objectives are strategic, and the methods to complete the mission and achieve the objectives are defined by the tactics, or tactical plan.

While strategy involves purpose, principle, and passion, tactics involve preparation, planning, and prioritization—the methods of achievement. Strategy is essential and helps ensure that we are all rowing in the same direction, working toward the same objectives, and guided by the same set of values. But if we stop there and say to ourselves, "I've done a good job by defining this strategy," what have we actually accomplished? The answer is "Absolutely nothing."

We must apply a series of tactics to use in achieving the vision and living out the purpose defined in our strategic plan. This tactical plan involves a lot of preparation for action, a lot of "how to" planning, and constant monitoring of priorities. Our strategy inspires us, and our tactics mobilize us. Our strategic objectives define what we are going to build, why we are going to build it, and the design requirements (blueprints)* for the objective. However, it is our tactical plan that defines the program, or operation. This program definition may include team selection, contractor utilization, project plans for who needs to be where and when, maybe even multiple projects within the program, budgets, what equipment or resources will be needed, as well as when and where it will be needed, etc.

> Tactics involve preparation, planning, and prioritization—the methods of achievement.

If you're a race-car team, this isn't quite the proverbial location where the rubber meets the road—that is the "action" phase discussed in the next chapter. This is where gas is put in the tank, maintenance schedules are planned out, budgets are defined, and the engine is started. You cannot get your race car out on the track without doing most of these tactical things first. And if you skip the items that aren't keeping you from getting on the track—like planning the maintenance, adjusting the suspension, and making sure you have the right tires for the conditions—your time on the track will be unproductive and short-lived, and may end in disaster.

---

* The design requirements are the "blueprints" for the effort. This is an analogy in which "blueprints" refers to the purpose, principles, and passion inspiring vision. In other words, the blueprints define the objective (what we want to build) and the guidelines (rules for how it will be built). In this analogy, we are comparing our lives, or the lives of our organizations, to a construction project.

Likewise, in almost everything worth doing, if we rush to action without taking any consideration for the tactical planning of how to perform properly, we are likely to be unproductive and short-lived. In some cases, this tactical planning step is so simple that it is done almost without realizing it and only takes a matter of seconds to complete. In more complex situations, the tactical planning may take days or weeks to complete but could shave months or years from the effort if given proper consideration in the beginning.

Preparation

Preparation is all about defining *how* we plan to accomplish our objectives. Again, note the link between the strategic and the tactical: we are preparing (tactical) to accomplish our objectives (strategic). This preparation will usually involve some form of study or practice, and it may involve defining a series of programs and projects. Benjamin Franklin is well known for saying, "By failing to prepare, you are preparing to fail."[1] Another famous American inventor, Alexander Graham Bell, put it this way: "Before anything else, preparation is the key to success."[2] In other words, if we want to succeed, we must first prepare for that task at hand.

Set things in order before taking action. Have a plan that guides your actions so that efficiencies are improved and results are achieved with greater yield. Part of this is program definition and project planning, and another part of it is team development. Make sure you have the right team in place to optimize the results and get the most out of the action to be invested.

> Have a plan that guides your actions so that efficiencies are improved and results are achieved with greater yield.

Sometimes it is easier to just jump straight into action, but when you do this, what do you accomplish? Did you accomplish anything with the effort? Did any accomplishment that may have occurred actually move you any closer to achieving your desired objectives, or did it just make you feel good about "doing something"?

What preparation does a football team go through prior to game time? There is physical conditioning of individual team members to ensure that they are capable of performing at the level required. They spend months doing practice drills to make sure everyone on the team knows every play in the playbook and has their timing down just right so the team functions as a synchronized unit.

Before the practice drills, they had to come up with the playbook in the first place. Someone thought through a set of plays, how they would be executed, and under what conditions they would be appropriate. They review countless hours of video on the competition for this game, making sure that they know the other team's habits and styles and what they are most likely to do in any given situation—and thus which plays in their playbook are most likely to have the desired outcome. All of this is tactical planning—preparing for the "battle."

None of this is actually doing anything on the playing field. None of this effort is producing a tangible result of winning a game. None of this effort is directly applicable to the action that takes place during the sixty minutes of game time on the field. Yet those who prepare most effectively before game time are most likely to succeed after the game clock starts ticking. This preparation may not be directly applicable, but it is most certainly indirectly applicable and absolutely essential.

In developing your own tactical plans, you must determine the essential steps needed for adequate preparation. You must develop your own "playbook," rehearse as needed, keep your skills sharp,

Tactics

define what projects are needed, and prepare effectively to execute these projects.

> You must develop your own "playbook," rehearse as needed, keep your skills sharp, define what projects are needed, and prepare effectively to execute these projects.

Planning

Planning and preparation are closely related yet still different parts of the process of tactics development. Preparing is about getting things in order, getting the right people in place, practicing and training as necessary, and aligning the right tools and resources for the job. Planning is taking the next step to develop a schedule, apply milestones and metrics, and coordinating the team and other resources that you've prepared in advance for this work. It's about developing action plans, goals, deadlines, decision gates, requirements, and deliverables.

A *plan* is documented, it is detailed, and it is accessible. It describes, in advance of action, a method, scheme, or program for achieving a particular objective or desired outcome to be reached in the future. It provides clarity. It is very specific about the schedule, or time frame, in which tasks must be accomplished. It defines not only what the tasks are but who is responsible for them and what the requirements are. It may also include some form of tolerances on the outcome that account for variances. These tolerances may take the form of a *target* objective, with a *threshold* that defines the minimally acceptable outcome, or possibly the definition of a best/worst/expected outcome.

Every plan is different, yet every plan has some basic core requirements that must be met in order to be effective. Here is a list of these core requirements that are common to all plans.

1. It is **written.**

    Writing down plans is important so that you can refer to them often during the execution of the plan. How can you follow a plan that you have not written down? More importantly, how can your team follow a plan that isn't communicated in writing? With today's modern technological conveniences, there are a number of ways to document a plan. It may be on paper, or it may be digital. It may be a paragraph, a drawing, or a project schedule. It may be a Gantt chart showing tasks, resources, predecessors, timelines, and more. It will often be a combination of many of these methods of documentation, but it must be documented and accessible to the team.

2. It is provided in **advance of action**.

    In other words, there is no such thing as a retroactive plan. A plan describes what you are *about to do*. It is like plotting a course on a map. If you plot where you went, you are recording history rather than planning the future. But if you plot out where you want to go, you have a plan for reaching a desired destination. You may run into obstacles that require you to take a detour, but you have a plan that will make your trip as efficient as possible.

3. It describes a **course of action**.

    It provides a course of action, or navigational route, from where you are to where you want to be. Where you want to be is your objective—it is the desired outcome to be reached in the future. Not only is the plan produced prior to action, but it is used throughout the action as a guide to help navigate the process. This is very important, whether you are developing a personal plan or a team plan. Personal plans help guide you and keep you focused on the target—keep you on course. If used properly, they will provide the necessary reminders to avoid distractions and help you reach your objectives. The same is true for team efforts with the added importance of communication. Anytime multiple people are working on the same course of action, the opportunity for confusion and divergent paths abounds. A well-developed, well-communicated, and well-coordinated plan minimizes that risk and allows the team to improve productivity.

4. It is precisely aimed at **specific metrics**.

Every plan must have very specific goals that are clearly defined—so you know when they've been met. These goals may include schedule deadlines, technical targets, milestones in the process, or other easily definable steps.

Keep in mind that it is important to make goals quickly achievable. In other words, break the plan down into enough finite goals that it is possible to meet a new goal with reasonable frequency. If it takes six months or a year to reach each goal, you and your team will likely get disheartened and lose focus. Keep that six-month goal, but add some thirty-day goals (maybe even weekly goals). This will help you measure progress better, and perhaps most importantly, it provides opportunity for early successes. Those early successes are great motivators that will inspire you, and your team, to focus on the longer-term successes that are needed.

5. It defines a *specific schedule, or time frame*.

You have to set deadlines for your plan—a schedule with time limits. The potential return on investment for any given project will have a timeline of value. If the project goes too long, its value diminishes.* If deadlines are missed, you need to reassess and determine if the task or project still offers sufficient value to continue. If not, drop it and move on to something of greater value. If so, keep at it and get it done as quickly as possible.

6. It **communicates the details**.

   It defines the course of action (what, when, how, and by whom). This is a critical component of the plan. Without it, your team doesn't know what to work on. The plan communicates what, when, how, and by whom so that the entire team can work effectively and efficiently.

   It also provides a source of accountability, which is also important. We all need to hold ourselves, and our teammates, accountable for properly executing the tasks that are assigned to them.

   Consider the plan for a particular play in a football team's playbook that calls for a receiver to run out fifteen yards and catch the football. The QB needs to trust that the receiver will be there. If the receiver stops at five yards, the ball is likely already in the air and will be intercepted by the competition. The same concept applies to any team situation. Everyone on the team needs to know the playbook and execute the plays correctly, or failure is inevitable.

7. It accounts for **variances**.

---

* A project's diminishing value over time is important to identify and understand. Perhaps a market will be missed, fees may be applied for late delivery, customer satisfaction may be reduced, a competitor may win the opportunity by delivering faster, the cost to execute may reach levels greater than the return expected, or you simply will miss opportunities to apply your time and resources to another project or task.

Tactics

Not every task is going to go according to plan. As a matter of fact, you'll find that in most cases, they won't go exactly according to plan. The plan should always account for a certain level of variances due to things that aren't foreseen and can't be tightly controlled. The plan should define the desired outcome, as well as the minimally acceptable outcome. It is best to also consider the likely outcomes of the effort. In other words, for each task in the process, define what is the expected outcome as well as the best and worst cases. After completing the plan, you'll then have the information necessary to manage the risks associated with the effort and discern whether the *worst-case* risk is acceptable.

Key Features of a Plan

1. It is **written**.
2. It is provided in **advance of action**.
3. It describes a **course of action**.
4. It is precisely aimed at **specific metrics**.
5. It defines a *specific schedule, or time frame*.
6. It **communicates the details**.
7. It accounts for **variances**.

Preparation does not necessarily define any of the key points listed in the previous paragraph, but a plan defines them all to some reasonable extent.

So our tactics involve preparation, planning, and prioritization. We've seen that preparation involves becoming ready for action— setting things in order. And our planning involves the definition of programs, or operations, that define how our mission will be accomplished. These programs must also include measurable goals that define the outcome in a recognizable manner, on a definite schedule or time frame. It is often helpful to define milestones along the path to reaching these goals. Milestones can help us judge progress more effectively and are a morale boost in that they provide a sense of accomplishment prior to reaching the final completion of the goal.

This brings us to the need for prioritization that clarifies the relative importance of varying tasks, goals, and even entire programs or operations.

Prioritization

Prioritization feeds into, and helps clarify, a plan. The steps in the plan (milestones and task items) often require a particular order. Sometimes this requirement is clear.[*] Sometimes the order is unclear and may not even fall out as a requirement from the project itself.[†] For instance, if a crane is needed for a construction project, there are certain tasks that clearly cannot be done prior to the crane being available. Yet the crane's availability may be driven by outside constraints not apparent to this project plan (e.g., it's being used on another project or has scheduled maintenance that must take place at a particular time).

Careful management of priorities is a must in any tactical plan. Priorities may shift during the course of the project. If a task gets behind schedule, it may increase in priority, for a time, in order to

---

[*] The need to prioritize milking the cow before pouring milk on your cereal is an example of clear priorities. Obviously a resource must be obtained before it can be utilized.

[†] Whether to prioritize milking the cow or collecting the eggs from the hen house is an example of priorities not necessarily mandated by the tasks themselves. If two resources will be needed in the future but neither is reliant on the other, the priority is not inherently defined. To prioritize these types of tasks, you'll have to look at critical path implications, external factors, and any interrelations with other tasks that may be on the critical path.

get it back on schedule. Another task may be ahead of schedule and thus have lower priority. Tasks in the critical path—the path of tasks that will delay the end goal if any individual task is delayed—will have the highest priority throughout the project, but what falls on this critical path may vary as conditions alter during the course of the project.

Dwight D. Eisenhower gave an address to the Second Assembly of the World Council of Churches held at Northwestern University in Evanston, Illinois, in 1954. In this address, he quoted an unnamed former president of the university as stating, "I have two kinds of problems, the urgent and the important."[3] Eisenhower went on to state to the audience that he believed, "Your being here can help place the important before us, and perhaps even give the important the touch of urgency."[4] From this quote, and the fact that Eisenhower's time-management skills were well thought of, sprang the concept of what is now commonly known as the Eisenhower Priority Principle.[5]

This principle grades every task, or call for your attention, as either important or not important and either urgent or not urgent. Because this principle yields four possible scenarios, it is often represented graphically with the four possible scenarios shown as the four quadrants of a two-by-two matrix. It has been repeated a myriad of times by many authors, coaches, and time-management gurus as an essential tool for prioritization. There are even several time-management software packages on the market that are built around this very concept. The four possible types of tasks are the following:

1. Urgent and important
2. Important but not urgent
3. Urgent but not important
4. Neither urgent nor important

Obviously this list is ranked in order of priority. If we assign a number value to each option such that urgency is either 0 (not urgent) or 1 (urgent) and importance is either 0 (not important) or 2 (important), we can take the sum of urgency plus importance to numerically rank the priority to place on the task. I like this numerical visualization because items that are neither important nor urgent are ranked 0. This provides a strong visual cue that we should invest zero time on these tasks.

Urgent and Important
Urgency + Importance = 1 + 2 = 3

Not Urgent but Important
Urgency + Importance = 0 + 2 = 2

Urgent but Not Important
Urgency + Importance = 1 + 0 = 1

Not Urgent and Not Important
Urgency + Importance = 0 + 0 = 0

Those things that are both urgent and important (1 + 2 = 3) must get our attention first. These are the unexpected emergencies or critical problems that pop up. If you witness a baby fall into a swimming pool, don't sit on your laurels and continue what you are doing. Take immediate action to rescue the child before it drowns! That is an urgent and important task. Applying this principle to our STAR model, the "action" and "results" are both applicable. You take action, and you get results. The problem is that the action is reactive rather than proactive. You aren't working on your plan; you're reacting to an emergency. It's important to address the emergency but get back to the plan as quickly as possible after addressing the situation.

The tasks that are important, but not urgent (2 + 0 = 2) are where we want to spend the majority of our time. These are things that we really need to be doing, but they don't have an immediately

Tactics

time-sensitive nature. Applying this to our STAR model, we note that all four aspects of the STAR are relevant. Developing our strategy, planning out our tactics, taking proactive action, and achieving results in accordance with the plans made are all important, but not urgent.

Note that by declaring these tasks to be "not urgent," we are simply observing that there isn't an "emergency" situation. We are not stating that there shouldn't be a sense of urgency associated with tasks in this situation. In fact, when the emergencies have been addressed, our sense of urgency should be dedicated to these tasks. We must apply a sense of urgency within our efforts, to tasks that are important but don't carry an automatic level of urgency in and of themselves. In other words, even though the task isn't urgent, because we know it is important, we will face it with a high sense of urgency and priority (interrupted only by those "emergencies" that really are both urgent and important).

Those tasks that are urgent but not important (1 + 0 = 1) make up the third priority category. The level of inherent urgency often causes these tasks to appear to be more important than they really are. For that reason, we will have to apply some of our resources to these tasks—mainly just to determine if they really are important. Once we determine that a task is unimportant, it should be relegated to the trash bin—or at least to the "get to it whenever we can" priority pile. If it isn't important, don't spend any more resources on it. If it will never become important; banish it from your to-do list entirely. If it may become important at some point, put it on reserve until it is important, but until then, don't waste resources on it.

The last category is neither urgent nor important (0 + 0 = 0). I don't think any explanation is necessary. Surely it is obvious that tasks that have no inherent level of urgency, and are completely unimportant, should simply be ignored. Don't invest any of your precious time or resources on these tasks.

STAR Performance

Remember the David and Goliath story I shared earlier. The threat presented by Goliath was that first category. It was both urgent and important. Action taken was reactive rather than proactive, but proactive time had already been spent planning for possibilities of this nature. David didn't hesitate; he already had a plan in place (proactive time). It is highly unlikely that David had ever thought of this exact scenario; however, he knew his purpose and principles well, he had great passion for what he believed in, and he knew his skill with a sling was at an expert level (tactical planning and preparation). In fact, his skills with the sling had been developed to handle unexpected threats. He may have envisioned lions, bears, and wolves, but the planning and preparation were equally applicable to the situation faced when he stood before Goliath.

As mentioned previously, he adapted his preexisting plan to the specifics of the current threat by picking up five stones, just in case Goliath's four relatives, or others standing nearby, decided to get in on the action. David spent most of his time and effort in the second category, which allowed him to be ready for the reactions needed to survive the first category emergencies.

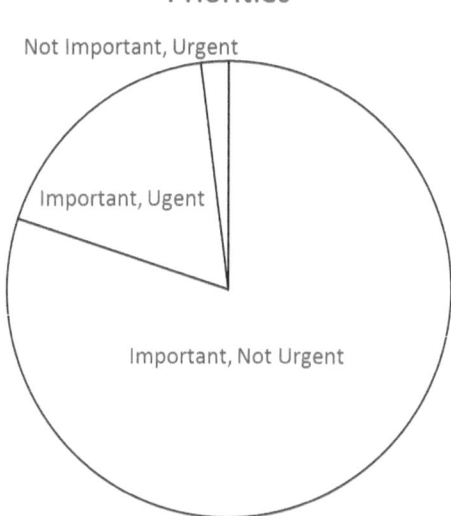

We can apply the old eighty/twenty rule to how we invest time in each priority category. With proper planning, we hope to keep first category emergencies to a minimum, but they are bound to happen at times. This category is so reactionary in nature that it doesn't leave time for planning, so any planning has to be done before the emergency presents itself. As a rule of thumb, I'd suggest planning to spend roughly 18 percent of your time in this category. The other 2 percent on the twenty side of the eighty/twenty rule is for the category of tasks that are urgent but not important. The only reason to invest any time in this category at all is simply to determine if the task is important. Sometimes urgent tasks can appear important even when they are not. As mentioned previously, apply just enough time to the task to determine its importance and, as soon as it is determined to be unimportant, get it off your list.

Our planning, both strategic and tactical, only exists in the second category. Planning is proactive; it is highly important but not immediately urgent. Again, it deserves the application of urgency in our proactive activity but doesn't demand immediate attention by nature of its inherent "emergency" status. This is where we want to spend at least 80 percent of our time. In an ideal world, we would spend 100 percent of our time here. However, we know that the world is not actually ideal, so it is wise for us to plan to spend some time on emergencies (and just a little time determining if an "emergency" really matters anyway).

Important and Urgent	
Time Investment	18 percent of our time
STAR Components	Action (reactive)
	Results (unplanned)

Important but Not Urgent	
Time Investment	80 percent of our time
STAR Components	Strategy
	Tactics
	Action (proactive)
	Results (planned)

Not Important but Urgent	
Time Investment	2 percent (just enough to validate importance)
STAR Component	none

Not Important and Not Urgent	
Time Investment	0 percent
STAR Component	none

Application

When we prepare appropriately, plan carefully, and prioritize effectively then our actions will be efficient and we'll make real, tangible progress toward our goals and objectives. Without taking these initial steps we'll have vague priorities that are shifting constantly in reaction to daily fires—often unimportant action that doesn't add value. Mahatma Gandhi once said, "Actions express priorities."[6] This is so true. Our true priorities are revealed by the action we take. If we do not define our priorities within our plans, then the "fires" of daily activity will tend to cause the priorities that capture our activity to sway and vary unnecessarily.

> When we prepare appropriately, plan carefully, and prioritize effectively, then our actions will be efficient and we'll make real, tangible progress toward our goals and objectives.

It is in the action phase where we start to see the results. Until that action is taken, nothing is really achieved, yet jumping into action without a plan and clear objectives is just treading water. Nothing is really achieved this way either. The proper course of action is to develop a strategy that we can really believe in, build a tactical plan around this strategy that defines a path to success, and then take action to execute this plan effectively. This way, our priorities will be sound and clearly reflect the goals and objectives we seek to achieve.

Our tactical plan defines how we plan to accomplish our strategic objectives. It provides a proper foundation for propelling forward in a successful manner. It mobilizes us, and our team, to take positive, focused, and well-coordinated action. This tactical plan includes preparation, planning, and priorities. These are three critical steps in the process that should not be overlooked.

Here are some quick pointers on how to put together your tactical plan:

1. preparation: setting things in order to prepare for action
    a. study: get to know the details of the task ahead
    b. train: keep important skills sharp, and improve or add to skills as needed
    c. identify: know what resources will be needed for the task ahead

d. team: make sure you have the right people on your team, and make sure that each person is in the right role to optimize team performance; add to the team if needed, and don't delay subtractions from the team that you know need to happen
2. planning: developing a specific action plan for how to move forward
   a. carefully plot out a detailed explanation of what needs to be done, when it should be completed, how to do it, and who is responsible for it
   b. create a schedule of tasks that applies milestones, metrics, and deadlines
   c. coordinate the team and other resources with the schedule, making sure resources will be available when they are needed
3. priorities: define a ranking of importance for objectives, goals, tasks, and milestones
   a. clarify the plan by defining and communicating the order of importance
   b. communicate with the team regularly and adjust priorities as needed, making sure the team knows immediately about any adjustments that are made

	Tactics
Prepare	readiness: setting things in order for upcoming action
Plan	how: the development of specific programs or operations that define how our mission will be accomplished
	goals: the measurable outcomes of a program or significant portion of a program
	milestones: intermediate stepping-stones along the path to completing a program.
Prioritize	first things first: defining a rank of importance for objectives and goals.

Remember PepsiCo's strategic plan reviewed in the previous chapter. I'd like to point back to this and review their tactical plan. We don't have access to the details of how they prepared and prioritized, although we can infer some of this from the documentation that is available. However, we do have access to descriptions of some of the programs, operations, or initiatives that are elements of the tactical plan. Recall that their mission was "to deliver top-tier financial performance while creating sustainable value for all stakeholders."[7] Their objectives were categorized as fitting into one of the following priorities: performance, human sustainability, environmental sustainability, or talent sustainability.

The plan defines a series of programs and initiatives that feed into one of these categories of objectives in fulfillment of their mission. For instance, under the *human sustainability* category, PepsiCo has several "product choice" programs including their "Saturated Fat Reduction Initiative," their "Added Sugar

STAR Performance

Reduction Initiative," their "Sodium Reduction Initiative," and their "Broadening Portfolio through R&D Innovations."[8]

They also define a number of partnerships, such as with the Healthy Weight Commitment Foundation,[9] Wholesome Wave,[10] GENYOUth Foundation,[11] and the Combia Water Center[12] that feed their multiple objective categories.

They define a series of resource conservation programs, alternative energy programs, sustainable farming initiative and initiatives for recycling, next gen materials, and waste reductions—all feeding the *environmental sustainability* objectives.[13]

For their *talent sustainability*, they have created a number of initiatives related to career opportunities, employee health, and community service. These initiatives include women in leadership, diverse supplier base, safety, health and wellness, human rights in the workplace, and global citizenship programs.[14]

Altogether, the report provides insight into PepsiCo's tactical plan for living out their strategy (purpose, principle, and passion) with a brief summary of their preparation, planning, and priorities.

Review

1. What are the three Ps of tactics?

2. What does preparation define?

3. What is the link between tactical (preparation) and strategic (objectives)?

4. What is planning, and how does it differ from preparation?

5. What are the seven core requirements common to all plans?

6. What are the four types of tasks according to the basic Eisenhower Priority Principle?

7. What are the numerical values assigned to each potential ranking of urgency and importance?

8. With these numerical values, what is the priority rating for each type of tasks noted in question 6?

9. How much of our time should generally be invested in the important but not urgent type of tasks?

10. Why would we spend any time on urgent but not important tasks?

Notes

---

1. "7 Must Read Life Lessons from Benjamin Franklin." BusinessInsider.com. December 31, 2014.
2. Quote first noted on poster in an office, then found referenced at "Alexander Graham Bell Facts." ScienceKids.co.nz. December 31, 2014.
3. Eisenhower, Dwight D. "Address at the Second Assembly of the World Council of Churches, Evanston, Illinois." August 19, 1954. Online by Gerhard Peters and John T. Woolley, *The American Presidency Project*. <http://www.presidency.ucsb.edu/ws/?pid=9991>.
4. Eisenhower, Dwight D. "Address at the Second Assembly of the World Council of Churches, Evanston, Illinois." August 19, 1954. Online by Gerhard Peters and John T. Woolley, *The American Presidency Project*. <http://www.presidency.ucsb.edu/ws/?pid=9991>.
5. "What Is Important Is Seldom Urgent and What Is Urgent Is Seldom Important." *Quote Investigator*. May 9, 2014. Web. July 8, 2015.
6. Easterby, Thea. "10 Thought Provoking Lessons from Mahatma Gandhi." *WriteChangeGrow.com*. January 2, 2015.
7. "PepsiCo Values." *PepsiCo Performance with Purpose: Sustainability Report 2013*. PepsiCo. Web. July 24, 2015, 1.
8. "PepsiCo Values." *PepsiCo Performance with Purpose: Sustainability Report 2013*. PepsiCo. Web. July 24, 2015, 11–16.
9. "PepsiCo Values." *PepsiCo Performance with Purpose: Sustainability Report 2013*. PepsiCo. Web. July 24, 2015, 12.
10. "PepsiCo Values." *PepsiCo Performance with Purpose: Sustainability Report 2013*. PepsiCo. Web. July 24, 2015, 19.
11. "PepsiCo Values." *PepsiCo Performance with Purpose: Sustainability Report 2013*. PepsiCo. Web. July 24, 2015, 23.
12. "PepsiCo Values." *PepsiCo Performance with Purpose: Sustainability Report 2013*. PepsiCo. Web. July 24, 2015, 32.
13. "PepsiCo Values." *PepsiCo Performance with Purpose: Sustainability Report 2013*. PepsiCo. Web. July 24, 2015.
14. "PepsiCo Values." *PepsiCo Performance with Purpose: Sustainability Report 2013*. PepsiCo. Web. July 24, 2015.

Chapter 4

Action

Practice | Persistence | Perspiration

An accomplished athlete has a finely tuned mind and body that is trained and strengthened to optimize performance in the sport of choice. In every body are multiple interworking systems—skeletal, respiratory, circulatory, muscular, nervous, and of course the mind that controls (or at least influences) all of the others. In an athlete, all of these systems are toned and strengthened—poised and practiced to work together in optimal efficiency.

In our own efforts to accomplish objectives and make progress in life, we have a proverbial "body" that must be tuned in a manner similar to the athlete's body. We are the mind of this body, and the results we achieve will depend highly upon the level of effort we put into it. This starts with our mental approach. Strategy is the skeleton that provides support, tactics is the circulatory and respiratory systems that provides energy and sustainment, and action is the muscular systems that keeps things moving.

As noted previously, if we stop at strategy or tactics, we never actually accomplish anything. Jumping straight to action increases the risk of accomplishing the wrong thing, or simply looking busy without actually accomplishing anything worthwhile. The point of developing strategy and tactics is to provide roots for our action enabling us to act intelligently with purpose, principle, and passion to achieve results that have value and merit.

> Strategy and tactics provide roots for our action, enabling us to act intelligently with purpose, principle, and passion to achieve results that have value and merit.

We can daydream and come up with a strategy filled with grand visions, but if we don't execute on this vision, it is just a dream. It is just something that we wish for. It's like planning to get rich from the lottery (without even buying a ticket). Joel Barker wisely put it this way: "Vision without action is merely a dream. Action without vision just passes the time. Vision with action can change the world."[1]

On the other hand, taking action without planning is busywork that has little, if any, value. It looks like work, but it isn't accomplishing much. If we want to create value, or as Mr. Barker puts it in the quote above, if we want to change the world, we have to have both vision and action. Taking it a step further, we have to have strategy, tactical plan, and action (STA …). Our action is defined by practice, persistence, and perspiration.

Practice

One important aspect of action is simply practice. The term *practice* can be interpreted two ways. The first is the act of rehearsing our actions to train ourselves to perform these actions with a higher degree of accuracy and efficiency when they matter

Action

most. This can be easily illustrated by the athlete that trains on the practice field to rehearse the playbook before actual game time. The second is the act of doing something and sticking with it until we get through it. Think of *practicing medicine* or *practicing law*. These concepts of practice invoke the idea of persistence and passion in the pursuit of an objective. Passion is strategic, but without action, it is lifeless. Imagine someone professing a faith but never acting on that faith. James, an Apostle in the Christian faith, wrote, "Faith by itself, if it does not have works, is dead."[2]

I'd like to suggest that the idea of *practice* here is a little of both the rehearsal of the playbook and executing the plays by sticking with a task until it is done. A sport offers clear opportunity for lots of practice. If you've ever been a part of an organized team in any sport, or a competitor in an individual sport, you know that practice is an important part of success. Practicing skills that are likely to be needed during a game is essential to keeping these skills ready for action. Practicing the playbook is also essential to having a team that works well together.

> Stop practicing, and you'll stop performing.

Life doesn't always provide such clear opportunities for rehearsing the playbook, but we can always find ways to keep our skills sharp. This might include reading, taking classes, attending seminars, or doing drills. If we don't pursue this kind of practice, then our skills weaken and we are more likely to make mistakes. We can't think that practicing a particular skill a single time means that we are done and are now experts at that skill. Practicing the skills we are likely to need in the pursuit of our objectives is an ongoing, everyday thing. Stop practicing and you'll stop performing. I love the word picture created by this Japanese proverb: "Learning through practice is like pushing a cart up a hill: if you slack off, it will slip backward."[3] Don't slack off on practicing or you'll lose ground, and your cart might just roll over you!

This concept is illustrated in the art of karate. A karate practitioner, referred to as a *karateka*, knows that expertise comes only after years of repeatedly performing the same motions. One of the grand masters of the art put the Japanese proverb about practice into his own words in forming one of the "Twenty Guiding Principles of Karate." "Karate is like boiling water: without heat, it returns to its tepid state."[4] This is true for any activity we pursue in life. Once a skill or capability is initially achieved, maintaining proficiency requires repetition, practice, and discipline. Without the effort of ongoing practice, the skill will be lessened, if not lost completely.

I learned to ride a bicycle as a child. To this day, I can still get on a bike and pedal around the neighborhood. But I don't practice this skill with diligent discipline. As a result, my proficiency is that of a casual rider. If I want to have the proficiency of a competitive rider or be able to take on challenging bike trails, I need to practice this skill daily and thus improve muscle tone, stamina, and form.

In the practice of karate, slow, rhythmic repetitions of *kata*[*] are intended to produce strength, flexibility, and muscle memory that result in the ability of the karateka to react instinctively when faced with a danger. These kata are repeated day after day, after day, for years, in order to achieve and maintain the capability of a karate master.

---

[*] Kata are prearranged sequential movements of stances, blocks, and strikes. In his book *The Essence of Okinawan Karate-Do* (Tuttle, 1976), Master Shoshin Nagamine states, "Kata can be described as a systematically organized series of defensive and offensive techniques performed in a sequence against one or more imaginary opponents, and given a symmetrical, linear pattern." This allows for a common platform of organized practice providing repetitive learning until the movements become instinctive.

Almost everyone has some level of familiarity with the black-belt system of signifying a karateka's level of skill and experience. Did you know that the black belt is like the zero point, with ranks below being "negative numbers" approaching zero. This is the ranking system of *kyu* and *dan* levels used in the arts of karate, judo, and tae kwon do.* In this system, the *kyu* rank represents the beginner level students. This is often broken up into a series of ranks (the exact number of *kyu* divisions used varies by school) from the novice, often represented by a white belt, to the more advanced, often represented by a brown belt. When a student is said to have mastered the basics sufficiently to really start learning the deeper truths of karate, he/she is promoted to the *dan* level or black belt.

> The more you sweat in practice, the less you bleed in battle.[5]

The *dan* level karateka teaches classes and mentors less-experienced karateka while training alongside contemporary black belts and under the direction of a master. Yet this black belt karateka will still consider themselves to be a student of the art. Even the sensei (teacher, typically *san-dan*, third-degree black belt, or higher) and *hanshi* (head master, or highest ranking member of the system; often a *ju-dan* or tenth-degree black belt) will tell you that they are students of the art. A very accomplished sensei recently told me that he was "learning" a kata that I was just being introduced to, despite the fact that he has many years of experience with that kata and has taught it to many students through the years. He told me that we would "learn together" as he showed me the kata.[6] In fact, the system's hanshi speaks often of the need to "just keep showing up," meaning that we have to

---

* The kyu and dan level ranking system originated with judo and was later adopted by karate and tae kwon do as a means of increasing the proliferation of these arts in society.

keep at it and keep coming to class if we are to grow and learn in the art.[7] He has been "showing up" for almost fifty years since he first started. He has the respect of the entire organization with dojos (training halls) all around the world[*] as being the master of the style, because he has continually practiced for such a long time—and continues to do so on a daily basis.

So to be proficient, just *keep showing up*. Formally practice and train as often as possible, and keep actively performing on a daily basis the actions and activities that are crucial to your long-term success so that your proficiency remains high. Whenever possible, seek out the guidance of a skilled master in the particular area to act as a mentor. Such mentors will provide opportunities to try things in a different manner and thus improve efficiencies or correct mistakes you may not even realize that you are making. When you practice continually, you will discover new possibilities, you will enlarge your circle of influence, and you will naturally grow as you become more confident and capable. You will become better at the skills you already possess, and you will find that you have an increasing capacity for learning new skills.

Persistence

The concept of practice, and "just showing up," lends itself beautifully to a segue into persistence. Almost anything and everything that is worth doing will be challenging. There will be obstacles, boundaries, and resistance to progress that you will face and have to overcome. Persistence will be required to get it done despite the obstacles. Sir Winston Churchill once addressed this need for persistence and perseverance when he said, "… never give in, never give in, never, never, never, never—in nothing,

---

[*] At the time of this writing, Ueshiro Shorin Ryu Karate dojos exist across the United States and internationally in Israel, Hong Kong, and New Zealand. http://www.shorinryu.com/dojo.htm accessed April 9, 2015.

great or small, large or petty—never give in except to convictions of honour and good sense."[8]

> Persistence is about seeking objectives in which we have confident conviction and doing whatever it takes to fulfill those objectives.

As a word of caution, there is a fine line between persistence and blind stubbornness. Don't be bullheaded about making course corrections in your plan. Our plans will often require adjustment along the way. Persistence isn't about sticking with a failing plan just because we're too proud to admit failure. Persistence is about seeking objectives in which we have confident conviction and doing whatever it takes to fulfill those objectives. That is what I believe Sir Churchill was referring to when he said never give in—except to convictions of honor and good sense. In other words, do what is right and honorable, and use discernment with "good sense" to adjust your plans as needed to achieve success.

When a plan starts to fail, adjust it or abandon it in favor of a better solution to achieving the objective. On rare occasions, we may need to abandon an objective itself because it may become obsolete, or we learn that it wasn't as valuable of an objective as we originally thought. Be careful not to be blind to this possibility, but also don't allow the obstacles and challenges to derail you from achieving a worthwhile objective—just because it was tough to accomplish.

Be persistent in the face of adversity. Don't let a challenge keep you from moving forward. Don't let opposition keep you from sticking with it. Nothing worth completing will ever be done without inspiring some level of opposition.

Stick with it! You'll find success in the end. Remember the story of Edison and the light bulb. It took many, many attempts to find the right combination of materials and design for it to work. Edison was not discouraged by all the failures. In fact, he was known for referring to them as successes in determining another configuration that wouldn't work. Napoleon Hill wrote, "Patience, persistence, and perspiration make an unbeatable combination for success."[9] Both Mr. Edison and Mr. Hill understood the importance of hard work, persistence in the effort, and patience to wait for the desired outcome. When you develop a similar awareness, you will become increasingly successful in your pursuits.

The fact is that it is often true that what we view as obstacles and hindrances are often the very things that strengthen us and enable us to do things differently, and thus improve and add value. There are two types of learning in life: *capitalization learning* and *compensation learning*. Capitalization learning is the art of capitalizing on something we are naturally gifted at in the first place—it is *building on the strengths we are naturally given*.[10] Compensation learning is all about working through, or around, the obstacles we face. It requires persistence. To learn in this manner, we must face our limitations and fears, get past our insecurities, and apply steadfast perseverance with an uncanny focus on the task at hand.[11] Don't let obstacles, or what might commonly be perceived as disadvantages, keep you from reaching your goals. These obstacles and *disadvantages* might actually be what develop within you the very abilities you need to excel.

Another story from history that emphasizes the importance of perseverance is that of the first-century Jewish sect known simply as "the Way." This sect taught a message of peace and hope in a restored relationship with the Almighty. They believed that the prophesied Messiah had come and that he had provided deliverance in a way that was rather unexpected. The deliverance was from the bondage of sin and a restored relationship with God, rather than the deliverance from political oppression and subjugation as many at the time expected. This Messiah had been a man named Yeshua,* and he also carried the name Emmanuel, which means "God with us." This relatively small sect of Judaism was rapidly expanding, and the members were faced with ostracism, hatred, persecution, and even torturous death from both the established religious courts of Judaism and the regional Roman government.

One of the sect's original leaders, a man by the name of James,† wrote a thesis to be delivered to the followers of the Way within the twelve tribes of Israel scattered around the known world. In his opening comments, he addresses the persecution and adversity that they faced and the importance to persevere in the face of such hardships because the purpose was more important than the obstacles. He states, "Let perseverance finish its work so that you may be mature and complete, not lacking anything" (James 1:4 ESV).[12]

His pep talk must have worked. The followers of the Way were filled with passion and a sense of purpose that was unstoppable. Their message eventually reached beyond Judaism and spread to the Gentile world by "adopting" Gentiles that believed in the message of the Way. The sect eventually lost the designation as

---

* Yeshua (עֵשׁוּיַ) was the Aramaic name that the Messiah would have commonly used. Much of the record of his life is recorded in New Testament writings that were predominantly written in Greek and thus used the Greek form of the name, Iesous (Ιησους). Centuries later, the Greek form was transliterated to English as Jesus, which is likely the most recognizable form of the name in the English language. The name Yeshua carries the meaning *Yahweh Saves* (Yahweh being the personal name for the God of Israel), indicating the purpose of the Messiah's life, death, and resurrection as bringing Yahweh's salvation to mankind.

† This thesis is now known as the book of James in the canon of the New Testament. It is likely the oldest of the New Testament writings, having been written between AD 40 and AD 50. The author is believed to be James, the brother of Jesus. (This information is found in the introductory notes to the book of James in the ESV translation of the Holy Bible).

followers of the Way and became known simply as "Christians"—taking on the likeness of the Greek version of the title Messiah (Christ), who is the Way.

In the first century, their followers grew exponentially—despite the intense obstacles.* Today Christianity is the most populace religion on earth, made up of nearly a third of the entire global population.[13] Regardless of your own personal thoughts on the faith of these followers of the Way, it cannot be overlooked that such a small group of disciples spread the message of the Way far and wide, despite rigorous persecution, intense obstacles, and heavy casualties, until their message became heard and accepted by a large population of the world. That is what perseverance, or *persistence*, is all about. Wouldn't you like to inspire that kind of persistence in those you lead?

Perspiration

Practice and long-term persistence, or perseverance, require dedication and hard work. It simply takes work to get things done. Good, old-fashioned effort. Sweat equity. When we are hampered by a fear of getting our hands dirty, putting in the extra effort, or just breaking a sweat, we miss out on much that life has to offer. Just as worthwhile objectives will require perseverance in the face of obstacles, it will require effort to accomplish. If it was easy, someone else would have already done it. Thomas Edison stated,

---

* Throughout history, many have attempted to hijack the banner of these people for their own political or power gain. Many have attempted, unsuccessfully, to destroy the band of followers. The Way was a sect of Judaism that was founded by a Jew (Yeshua), led by a team of Jewish followers, and made up of Jewish believers. As their message spread beyond Judaism, they "grafted" Gentiles into the Jewish "vine" to make them of "one body." As the name transitioned from the Way to "Christians," the distinction between Jew and Gentile follower became less and less defined until it is no longer commonly thought of as a sect of Judaism—yet that is exactly where Christianity, "the Way," actually comes from.

Action

"Opportunity is missed by most people because it is dressed in overalls and looks like work."[14] This is a somewhat comical way to say that we often miss opportunities that are staring us in the face simply because we aren't willing to do the work needed to take advantage of them.

Sacrifice will almost always be required of us when pursuing worthy objectives. We will have to sacrifice time, energy, money, comfort, and convenience to get things done. Don't be afraid of the sacrifices required, because in the end, the reward will be worth the effort. Of course this is the very reason that the concepts of purpose, principle, and passion are so fundamentally important. Without a sense of purpose and vision that inspires passion for the cause, how do we expect to maintain any sense of motivation to persist in the face of intense obstacles?

In the athletic arena, the concept of perspiration can be clearly seen. When an athlete or team doesn't put in the effort with passion and commitment, it is evident on the field. It is a thrill to watch a football game with two highly talented, well prepared teams going at the competition with intense passion and excitement. These types of games can often come right down to the final seconds before the winner is decided. As a great example, Super Bowl XLIX was just such an exciting contest. I wasn't a true fan of either team, but both teams were good, and they both played the entire game with intense passion and an obvious desire to win. There was a lot of perspiration driven by hard work that had been undergirded by a lot of preparation. The game could literally have gone either way, right up until the last twenty-six seconds of the game. That is the kind of game that is exciting to watch.

If you want to succeed without doing the hard work, buy a lottery ticket and hope you are the one-in-a-billion winner who gets rich by the luck of the draw. For the rest of us, we've got to be willing to put in the time and effort to make it happen the old-fashioned way. We've got to earn it through hard work. As

Thomas Edison so eloquently pointed out, "Genius is one percent inspiration, ninety-nine percent perspiration."[15]

Application

Action is about putting meat on the bones of the skeleton created by strategy and tactical plans. It is the doing that gets the plans accomplished. It will require practice, persistence, and perspiration.

	Action
Practice	rehearsing: refers to the act of rehearsing the plan (e.g., practicing the playbook, or practicing your lines)
	doing: refers to the act of direct and ongoing participation in the plan (e.g., practicing medicine)
Persistence	showing up: steadfast dedication to the mission even in the face of adversity and obstacles
Perspiration	hard work: diligent, focused hard work

Practice is about both rehearsing and continually doing. It's about rehearsing our plans and keeping them in clear focus at all times. It's also about sticking with a task until it's done. Repetition and discipline are required to achieve and maintain the skills needed for success. Persistence in the face of adversity and challenge is essential. You've got to just keep showing up if you want to accomplish anything worthwhile. It will require your willingness to do whatever it takes to fulfill the objectives within the boundaries of your predefined principles. Perspiration kind of speaks for itself. Getting things done will require diligent, focused hard work. Once the plan is set, just get to it.

Action

When we combine practice, persistence, and perspiration in the actions that we embark upon, we will become unstoppable. This type of action must be modeled from the top down. When modeled sincerely, it radiates with infectious passion that will impact every person you work with and will transform your entire organization into a powerhouse of high-value activity and meaningful results.

STAR Performance

Review

1. What are the three Ps of proactive action?

2. What are the two interpretations, or applications, of the term *practice*?

3. Fill in the blank. Stop practicing, and you'll stop _____.

4. What is persistence in our actions?

5. Why is persistence important to success?

6. What do we mean by *perspiration*?

7. What is almost always required of us when pursuing a worthy objective?

Notes

1. "Action." Values.com. The Foundation for a Better Life. Web. April 9, 2014.
2. "James 2:17." The Holy Bible, English Standard Version. Crossway. 2001.
3. As quoted in Funakoshi, Gichin. And Genwa Nakasone. *The Twenty Guiding Principles of Karate: The Spiritual Legacy of the Master.* Kodansha USA. 2012 (originally published in 1938).
4. Funakoshi, Gichin. *The Twenty Guiding Principles of Karate: The Spiritual Legacy of the Master.* Kodansha USA. 2012.
5. Anonymous.
6. Instructional comment from Sensei Kurt Tezel, *Godan* (fifth-degree black belt) in the Ueshiro Shorin Ryu Karate style, during kata training.
7. Comments from Hanshi Robert Scaglione, *Judan* (tenth-degree black belt) in the Ueshiro Shorin Ryu Karate style. This comment is repeated at nearly every gathering of karateka he attends. See http://www.shorinryu.com/hanshibio.htm for his bio.
8. Churchill, Winston. "Never Give In." Address to Harrow School. Harrow School, London. October 29, 1941. Speech. © The Estate of Winston S. Churchill.
9. Hill, Napoleon. *Think, and Grow Rich.* Pacific Publishing Studio. 2009.
10. Gladwell, Malcolm. *David and Goliath: Underdogs, Misfits, and the Art of Battling Giants.* Little, Brown and Company. New York. 2013, 112.
11. Ibid, 113.
12. "James 1:4." The Holy Bible: New International Version. Biblica. 2011.
13. "The Global Religious Landscape." *The Pew Forum on Religion and Public Life.* Pew Research Center. December 18, 2012. Reports Christianity as the largest religious group with 31.5 percent of the global population.
14. "Thomas Edison Quotes." ThomasEdison.com. Gerald Beals, 1996. Web. January 2, 2015.
15. "Thomas Edison Quotes." ThomasEdison.com. Gerald Beals, 1996. Web. January 2, 2015.

Chapter 5

Results

Patience | Productivity | Probing

We've talked about building a strategy that clearly defines purpose, sets principles that are to be adhered to, and communicates a vision that fills you and your team with passion. We've addressed the need to develop tactical plans for how to accomplish the objectives defined by the vision. And we've addressed the need to put all of these foundational layers into real-world application with persistent action. Now that the action is well underway, what do we expect to come of it, and how do we know when it has been accomplished?

Getting to these results will require a bit of patience, a focus on production, and continual probing to see how we are doing and what course corrections might be needed. The completion of the task is far more important than the start of the task. There is an ancient Hebrew proverb that states, "The end of a matter is better than its beginning, and patience is better than pride."[1]

This proverb speaks to the fact that finishing, or completing, a task is far better than beginning a task. Obviously every finished task has a beginning, so we must start if we are to finish. But not all things begun are seen through to completion. It also speaks to the importance of attitude and patience, noting that a spirit of patience is of greater value than a spirit of pride.*

Patience

Obviously the goal is almost always to reach our objectives in the shortest possible time, with the fewest possible resources. Patience is about being realistic in these expectations. It is not an excuse for laziness to be used when schedules are not met, but it is a requirement for setting schedules that are realistic. You can't expect a runner to finish a marathon in fifteen minutes. The fastest runner alive won't even come close to that expectation. Whatever your program of effort, don't expect results to take shape faster than is reasonably possible.

Expectations should be set in the planning stages. These tactical goals or deadlines are important, and every effort should be made to focus on them. A common management mistake is forcefully pushing unrealistic goals and deadlines on a team. This demoralizes the team, because they know the goals are unrealistic and it disappoints the manager and because they convince themselves the goal will be met, until it isn't.

There is a management philosophy that suggests that the way to reach goals in the shortest amount of time is to set deadlines that are overly aggressive, knowing that they won't be met but assuming that the aggressive schedule will keep the pressure on the team so they are more likely to meet the "real" deadline that went unpublished. While this may work on occasion, I

---

* Some translations use the term "arrogance" in place of "pride" for the Hebrew word *gabah*, meaning "lofty, proud, haughty, boastful, or arrogant."

personally do not believe that it is in the best interest of the team or organization. Even if it works on a given project, it is not likely to work repetitively and will cause burnout, high turnover, or malaise on your team. Not to mention the fact that if your team requires this type of bullying to get anything done, then you've got the wrong people on your team! If you are setting unrealistic expectations and resorting to this type of bullying to compensate, then you may be the wrong leader for the team.

If your team is honest with you, they will push back like Scotty pushed back when Captain Kirk tried to tell him he had less time than required to get something done. "I cannae change the laws of physics! I've got to have thirty minutes!"*[2] Years later, Scotty mentored a younger Chief Engineer La Forge by telling him, "Starship captains are like children. They want everything right now and they want it their way. The secret is to give them what they need, not what they want."†[3] I know that this is a fictional character and fictional situations, but it illustrates my point. We can, and should, push ourselves and our teams to be, and do, the best possible. And we must accept the reality of the situation while being patient to set expectations for results on a reasonable and achievable schedule. If we do not, all we will accomplish is the formation of a dishonest set of principles, a culture of misrepresentation of facts, an attitude of ambivalence toward published deadlines and requirements, and a downtrodden team that expects failure on every project.

You can't expect your team to be honest with you about anything if you aren't honest with them about everything—including deadlines and requirements. Such dishonesty is a recipe for disaster and a setup for failure. Some failures can be good because they teach us something important, but if our impatience

---

* This comes from the original *Star Trek* TV series episode "The Naked Time."

† This comes from *Star Trek—The Next Generation* episode "Relics."

predetermines failure, it is of no value whatsoever. In fact, it's actually a value killer and team destroyer.

> Time is the universal currency. You can't get things done without it.

It is a simple fact of life that any effort worth doing will take some amount of time. Time is the universal currency. You can't get things done without it. Ignoring this fact will not prove productive or rewarding. Rather it will prove frustrating and disappointing. The hugely successful businessman Warren Buffett once said, "No matter how great the talent or efforts, some things just take time. You can't produce a baby in one month by getting nine women pregnant."[4] He was clearly using colorful imagery to making a jovial impression while establishing the fact that patience is essential. *Some things just take time.*

On the other hand, taking too much time to accomplish your goals will be equally as frustrating and disappointing. Some projects have hard and fast deadlines set by external constraints. If these deadlines simply cannot be met by the project at hand, perhaps an alternate approach is needed—or the project should be abandoned altogether.

If a product-development project is going to take so long to complete that the window of opportunity in the market place will not be met, then the project should be avoided. You may seek an alternative path to market such as removing some of the requirements if doing so will reduce the development cycle without eliminating your product from the market. You may choose to come up with a different product, or maybe a partnership with another product provider that you can rebrand and adapt for the targeted market. You may simply walk away from this project altogether if an acceptable means to meet the goal cannot be found. But if you simply push forward with an unrealistic and unattainable goal, what do you stand to gain from the effort?

Make sure that all parties involved have a clear understanding of the time investment required to achieve the goal before you start, as well as all external factors that impact the schedule requirements. Avoid producing surprises by clarifying all expectations and requirements as much as possible, and clearly communicating any changes to those requirements that may occur along the way.* A common set of expectations is essential to having a productive and fruitful team. When you are patient in this way, you will energize your team and accomplish so much more than you ever thought possible.

Productivity

At the end of the day, some level of productivity—the production of real, tangible results—is what we are after. By productivity, we simply mean the ability to deliver something of value and a measure of the efficiency with which it is delivered. Our strategy gives meaning, our tactics give direction, our action provides progress, and our results yield productivity. If we aren't being productive, then what's the point in all the planning and effort? Henry Ford noted, "Vision without execution is just hallucination."[5]

> Our strategy gives meaning, our tactics give direction, our action provides progress, and our results yield productivity.

---

* Common changes that occur midproject are driven by things like developers learning that the intended design path won't work, sales learning of a shift in the market window, or management learning of a change in available funding. There are many possible drivers for such changes, and it will be impossible to identify all possibilities from the start, so frequent and open communication throughout the project is essential.

Every vision describes an objective, or a set of objectives. These objectives are what you are intending to accomplish. A tactical plan breaks this vision down into measurable goals and milestones. This provides a means by which to measure progress toward the objective. It is certainly possible to stay extremely busy with a flurry of action. Is the action actually moving you toward your goals? Could you make similar progress with less effort? Could you make significantly more progress with the same effort? Productivity is a measure of both what we produce and how efficiently we produce it.

Make certain that you know what you are striving to achieve, and make certain everyone on your teams knows the goals as well as you do. These clearly defined goals are essential to being productive. Without the goals, how would you know if you had produced the desired outcome? How would you know what the desired outcome actually was?

In addition to clarifying the desired outcome with goals, you'll want to reflect on the efficiency with which the goals were reached. Even if you finish within the defined schedule, you may find ways to do it more efficiently next time. This will impact your team by giving them an awareness of performance possibilities that they did not image were possible, as they improve, excel, and flourish in the results that they achieve.

Probing

If we are honest with ourselves, we will note that there is always opportunity for improvement. There's always a more efficient way to do something, always an opportunity to be faster, less expensive, better quality—or some combination of these improvements. Never settle for how things are, but always monitor and reflect on ways to improve. This monitoring and reflecting is probing the results. Once again, Henry Ford shared some insightful thoughts on this when he stated, "The only real mistake is the one from which we learn nothing."[6]

Results

> If we are honest with ourselves, we will note that there is always opportunity for improvement.

In the production quality and continuous improvement arena, there is a well-known and commonly used acronym, DMAIC, which refers to a "five-phase improvement cycle" (pronounced "deh-MAY-ihk").[7] It is a "data-driven quality strategy used to improve processes."[8] This acronym refers to five critical steps of process improvement: define, measure, analyze, improve, and control. The DMAIC model is an extension of the PDCA model for quality improvement first introduced by W. Edwards Deming. Deming suggested that the way to continually improve quality (and thus performance) is to plan, do, check, and then act.

The *plan* phase involves an assessment of current performance and the identification of opportunities for improvement. This requires data collection, root cause analysis, and the development of a plan for implementation of a potential solution, and a means to test the solution once implemented. The *do* phase involves implementing the planned solution—often on a prototype or pilot scale before "across the board" implementation. *Checking* is about measuring the results to see if it actually solved the problem or took steps toward a solution. The *acting* phase is about making changes based on the checks that were made. Broaden the scope of implementation, if appropriate, or revise the plan and retest by going through the model steps again as needed. This PDCA process can be (and should be) repeated over and over to continually improve processes, procedures, designs, and overall performance.[9]

This mantra of continuous improvement is extremely similar to what I mean when I say, "Probe." We must be continually probing ourselves, our plans, our actions, and our results if we are to successfully achieve improvements in our performance. We can't do something better if we don't know what it is we did in the first place or how well we actually did it. When we do know how well we did, we will begin to discover ways to do it better and start to generate the improvements that impact our bottom line every day.

This begins with the "define" portion of the DMAIC process, which is essentially our tactical plan. It communicates goals, timelines, critical requirements, and scope of work.* Once the action begins, we can measure all critical aspects of the effort.† Initially we are establishing a baseline for comparison, and in some cases, a baseline for comparison may exist in prior efforts (either our own efforts or those of others). We may be comparing that baseline to a target level of performance, or we may be developing a baseline from which we intend to improve without having a known target. As time, and action, progresses, we want to achieve improvements from these baselines. These improvements may come in the form of reduction in the cost to perform a task or

---

* My definition of the define phase as similar to the tactics phase is based on the definition of the define phase provided in Pande et al. They state that the define phase is about identifying the problem(s), defining requirements, setting goals, and clarifying the scope.

† Our action phase and results phase will have significant overlap—both being part of the remaining steps in the DMAIC cycle. As action progresses and we begin to see results, we will *measure* these results, *analyze* what we've measured, develop *improvement* plans, and implement *controls* to continue monitoring and correcting. Pande et al. provide the following definitions for the MAIC portion of the DMAIC cycle: *measure* = validating the problem or process, measuring performance, refining the problem or goal, measuring key inputs, and gathering efficiency data; *analyze* = develop and validate causal hypothesis, identify "best practices," identify "vital few" root causes, assess process design (look for bottlenecks, alternate paths, etc.), and refine requirements; *improve* = develop ideas to remove root causes, redesign process or design a new process (challenge assumptions, apply creativity), test solutions and measure results and standardize those that work; *control* = establish standard measures and reviews to maintain performance and implement corrective action as needed.

produce a widget, or in the time or resources it takes to complete the action.

This will often take a lot of analysis of the measurements we made. We have to ask questions—lots of questions. Why did it take this long to complete the task? What resources could have been applied to expedite delivery? How could we have done the same work with fewer resources? The level of detail and complexity of this analysis will depend on the type of action or process we are working on, and the priority level determined for finding improvements.

> Failures are really lessons on improvement, unless we don't learn from them ... Then they are just failures.

The aim is to achieve real improvements that add value and streamline our processes. We want to get better at what we do—no matter what tasks, projects, or processes we are referring to. A manufacturing manager wants to increase yield and decrease cost on the production line. A supply chain manager seeks to improve inventory cycle times and delivery lead times. An engineer wants to improve development cycle times while reducing the resources required to get it done. A homemaker seeks to better balance the multitasking requirements of childcare, meal production, pantry stocking, housekeeping, laundry service, transportation, and educational development. You see, no matter what your particular vision, or the specific actions you are working on, the opportunity to probe results and find ways to improve efficiencies and productivity is always there. When you capitalize on this opportunity, you will accomplish more and experience increased satisfaction with your results.

So remember, as results begin to flow from our actions, we need to monitor them, measure them, and analyze them in order to improve them. Some results will be good, and can always be improved. Some results will be bad, and we need to understand them and learn from the mistakes so we can make appropriate course corrections. Failures are really lessons on improvement, unless we don't learn from them … Then they are just failures.

I would also like to point out that, while identifying and admitting problems is the first step, coming up with potential solutions is critical. As a leader, I often find that those around me (and often myself, if I'm brutally honest) are fond of pointing out problems. These problems might be mistakes someone made, or something that was overlooked, of something that could have been done better, or any number of categories of problems. I've had days when there was literally a line outside my office door—sometimes backed up down the hallway—with people reporting problems. Usually these reports of problems are not accompanied by a solution.

When this occurs, I thank the team member for bringing the problem to my attention and ask them to present a solution to the problem. Common responses to the request for a solution are "I'm not to blame for this" or "I'm not the expert at finding a solution to this." My response to these comments is simple. I'm not interested in placing blame, but I am interested in fixing the problem. Of course if negligence or sabotage is the reason for the problem, then I am interested in placing blame because the solution is removing the culprit, but this is the exception, not the rule. Generally problems occur because of an honest mistake or an inefficient process, and placing blame just gives the team an excuse to avoid a real solution.

Never hide a problem, but when reporting a problem, always come with a proposed solution, several solution options to choose from, or at least a plan for how we will look for a solution. If you report a problem without a solution or suggested path to a solution, I'm likely to delegate the task of coming up with a solution to you anyway. So start with the assumption that the problem must be reported, and you'll need to present a path to a solution.

Application

To apply what we've discussed in this chapter, start with patience. Remember that you can't expect things to happen faster than is realistically possible. Be aggressive, but maintain realistic expectations for yourself, and for your team. Be careful not to substitute laziness for patience by claiming to be patient as an excuse for what is really just being lazy. Both impatience and laziness are performance killers.

Results	
Patience	waiting on results: having realistic expectations
Productivity	execution: ability to bring forth goods or services; the execution of vision
Probing	introspection: monitoring progress, asking the tough questions, and implementing corrective actions when necessary

You will also need to focus on productivity. You've got to be delivering on the demands of your plans, or the plans will not be achieved. Results yield productivity—good or bad. Make sure that you, and everyone on your team, know the goals and objectives, work tirelessly toward them, and are focused on ongoing improvements in efficiencies.

Focusing on these improvements will require you to be honestly introspective and searching for opportunities to improve. There is always room for improvement. Learn where improvements will provide the greatest impact to overall objectives and put in the effort to monitor and improve. Implement a process, such as DMAIC, that will help you and your team see how you are doing, analyze the results achieved, identify opportunities for improvements, and implement changes that make things better.

STAR Performance

Review

1. What are the three Ps of results?

2. What is patience? What is it not?

3. What is the universal currency?

4. How do we define productivity?

5. Fill in the blanks. Our strategy gives _____, our tactics give _____, our action provides _____, and our results yield _____.

6. What two things are measured by productivity?

7. What is "probing the results"?

8. What does the acronym DMAIC represent, and how does it apply to probing the results?

9. What are failures?

Notes

---

1. "Ecclesiastes 7:8." The Holy Bible: New International Version. Zondervan. 2011.
2. "Montgomery Scott." *Memory Alpha*. Wikia. Web. February 24, 2015. <http://en.memory-alpha.org/wiki/Montgomery_Scott>.
3. Ibid.
4. Taibi, Catherine. "The 16 Best Things Warren Buffett Has Ever Said." *The Huffington Post*. TheHuffingtonPost.com. Web. January 13, 2015.
5. "Henry Ford: 'Vision without Execution Is ...'" Changemakrs.com. Web. January 14, 2015.
6. Andersen, Erika. "21 Quotes from Henry Ford on Business, Leadership and Life." Forbes.com. *Forbes Magazine*, May 31, 2013. Web. January 14, 2015.
7. Pande, Peter S., Robert P. Neuman, and Roland R. Cavanagh. *The Six Sigma Way*. McGraw-Hill. New York, 2000, 37.
8. "The Define Measure Analyze Improve Control (DMAIC) Process." *DMAIC Approach*. American Society for Quality. Web. January 14, 2015.
9. Pande, Peter S., Robert P. Neuman, and Roland R. Cavanagh. *The Six Sigma Way*. McGraw-Hill. New York, 2000, 37.

Chapter 6

Performance

Strategy | Tactics | Action | Results

Performance implies both the accomplishment of an objective and the efficiency with which the objective is met. It is, thus, closely related to productivity. In our context, "productivity" is a measure of results, while "performance" is a measure of the entire process—including results. Performance encompasses both the planning and the doing. Productivity is a measure of the doing—the results achieved through our actions—while performance is a measure of the accomplishment of our objectives, the effectiveness of the planning, the efficiency of the action, and the improvement of results over time.

In other words, when we say "performance," we are talking about getting things done, as well as the efficiency with which these things are done. In this way, it is closely related to both action and results while drawing directly from strategy and tactics.

The intended purpose of all of our effort is defined by our strategy, with a path to this intended purpose being outlined in our tactics. Our action involves practice, persistence, and perspiration—another way of saying *the accomplishment of objectives*. Our results require patience, productivity, and probing—another way of saying *the efficiency of the action and the improvement of results over time*. In this way, performance is defined, measured, judged, and achieved via our STAR methodology (unified strategy, tactics, action, and results).

> Performance is defined, measured, judged, and achieved via our STAR methodology (unified strategy, tactics, action, and results).

Precepts

Remember the example given previously of the karate students and how important practice is to their development? I'm going to borrow another concept from the philosophy of Okinawan karate. There are four precepts taught as a means of building a "warrior spirit." The precepts are *gan, soku, tanden,* and *riki*.[1] These four precepts can be visualized as analogous to the precepts of STAR Performance: strategy, tactics, action, and results.

Gan	
Eye	awareness, perception, visualization, concentration;
Strategy	awareness of purpose, perception of vision, adherence to values or principles
Soku	
Foot	strong foothold, balance, foundation, readying the fist;
Tactics	strong plan of action, balance of priorities, readying the team

Tanden	
Stomach/Gut courage, spirit, attitude;	
Action	the courage to take action, the drive to fuel the perspiration that comes with hard work, and the persistence to stick with it despite obstacles

Riki	
Power	Strength, power, delivery;
Results	powerful delivery of solid action toward a sound plan

Gan

The word *gan* literally means "eye," and figuratively refers to perception or awareness, intuition, hunch, instinct—a way of seeing, judging or understanding something. To a karateka, gan refers to the physical awareness of surroundings, a visualization of the desired outcome, and the perception of character that controls one's influence on surroundings.

Character development is central to karate. Dojos, or karate training halls, will typically have a set of dojo rules that the karateka (students) are expected to follow. In many of the dojos that I have seen, the first and last rules are the same: always show courtesy to all.[2] Courtesy is thus the beginning and ending of karate training. This comes from the teaching of Master Funakoshi, "the father of modern day karate," who taught twenty guiding principles of karate. The first principle that he taught is "Do not forget that karate-do begins and ends with 'rei.'"[3] By way of explanation, "'rei' is often defined as 'respect,' but it actually means much more. 'Rei' encompasses both an attitude of respect for others and a sense of self-esteem … True 'rei' is the outward expression of a respectful heart."[4] Another early master of the art states, "Karate begins with courtesy and ends with it … We must first purify our minds and always be mentally and physically sound."[5] Courtesy is a way of seeing life and our interactions with others that is fundamental to traditional Okinawan karate. It is said that "a good warrior never enters onto the battlefield to fight, but to right a wrong."[6] That is living a life with character and with selfless purpose.

> Visualization of the desired outcome is key in any confrontational or competitive situation.

Visualization of the desired outcome is key in any confrontational or competitive situation. If you cannot envision a successful outcome, run away as fast as possible! Ask any professional athlete and they will tell that the first step is visualizing success. A basketball player must visualize the ball going through the hoop before taking the shot. A quarterback visualizes the ball landing in the arms of his receiver. This visualization alone will not guarantee success, but without this visualization, it is almost guaranteed that success will not be achieved.

Physical awareness of surroundings is equally important to the karateka—and to everyone else for that matter. The person that is distracted by a text message while they are driving is demonstrating horrible awareness that may have lethal consequences. The concept of defensive driving in which one continually monitors the road ahead, and employs sweeping glances into mirrors along with peripheral vision to be aware of all that is happening on the road around them, demonstrates gan, or a strong awareness of surroundings.

The strategy component to *STAR Performance* involves purpose, principle, and passion. Strategy is an awareness of purpose, an adherence to values or principles, and a strong perception of vision and direction. The karateka's visualization of a desired outcome is analogous to the development of a vision that inspires passion. If we want to achieve something specific, we have to know what that something specific actually is, and we have to have a passion for achieving it. That is vision.

> Strategy is an awareness of purpose, an adherence to values or principles, and a strong perception of vision and direction.

The implementation of character is the embodiment of principle. We all have character and principles—they may be good or bad in nature. Our principles may push us to benefit the world around us or simply drain it for our own selfish gains. How we apply principles to living, and the actions we take—whether on an individual level or corporately—defines our character.

Soku

The term soku means leg or foot. By implication, it refers to being sufficient.[7] In other words, it refers to being well balanced with a strong foundation or base—sufficient and prepared for the task at hand. In karate class, the teacher will repeatedly give the instructions to "step first."[8] Stepping first refers to the need to get your feet anchored in position before delivering a block or strike because the feet are the roots that anchor your body and provide stability. This is soku. It is the concept of rooting down, gripping the ground, and lowering your center of gravity to become immovable, distributing your weight and foot placement for a strong base and maximum stability.

Think of a race car. The suspension and tires are designed to cause the vehicle to grip the road. The aerodynamics of the car can work against the driver by creating lift that reduces how well the vehicle grips the road—thus reducing traction and control, or maybe even tossing the vehicle into the air. Race cars and high-powered sports cars will use spoilers and custom body shapes to promote down force. A spoiler is basically a wing, or flap, that generates lift toward the ground (down force) rather than away from it. This pushes the vehicle down, onto the ground, to allow it to maintain a firm foundation giving it better cornering speed.[9]

Many race cars have crashed as a result of this phenomenon. NASCAR vehicles racing at speeds in excess of 195 mph can generate enough lift to pick the car up if they spin out. To avoid this problem, engineers devised a rooftop flap that lifts when the pressure on the roof of the vehicle drops sufficiently. The flap lowers lift, much like the flaps on an aircraft wing, so that the car is no longer lifting off the road.[10]

They go to all this trouble because down force is essential to safety, to proper vehicle control, and to efficiently moving around the track. For the karateka, *down force* is about gripping the deck (ground) for maximum stability. Applied to projects, business ventures, and life in general, this *down force*, or foundation, is all about having a strong plan of action that balances priorities and readies the team for action. This is exactly what our tactical planning portion of the *STAR Performance* model is all about. Set your foundation, root down, grip the deck, and prepare for a bolt of action.

Tanden

Tanden is literally translated as abdomen, belly, or stomach. In the oriental culture from which martial arts developed, the term *tanden* refers to the physical, mental, and emotional center of the body. Physically it is the center of gravity. Your soku is the foundation that supports the body, and your tanden is the very center of mass that this soku must support. It is also viewed as the source of energy (qi or ki). Deep, full breathing that pulls oxygen into the tanden will fuel the body and mind, providing the dichotomy of both relaxation and energy.

Tanden is about spirit. Not in the religious, spiritual sense but in reference to the spirit or attitude to succeed, the drive to win, and the motivation to pour everything you've got into the action to be taken. It is said that "it is always the hungriest fighter who wins."[11] The team with the strongest passion is generally the victor in any competition. In a fight, the one most motivated is generally the one that wins.

To visualize this, I think of two types of physical confrontation situations that I could be involved in. Let me clarify that I do not believe that physical fighting is ever the best means of solving our differences. Coming to blows over our differences doesn't solve the issue. Instead it buries the problem, and future resurfacing is often inevitable. A healthy debate or confrontation, on the other hand, is beneficial. The constructive criticism of a good coach seeking to guide you to perform better is an example of healthy confrontation. Children screaming at each other in anger over a toy they both want to play with is unhealthy confrontation.

My primary passion is for making peace. Healthy debate and confrontation is a normal stepping-stone on the path to peaceful resolution of our differences, and to finding the most effective solution to our problems. When confrontation moves beyond friendly debate and into fighting, it loses its value and becomes destructive. Fighting, by my definition, is thus the use of physical or verbal assaults in unhealthy and destructive confrontation, rather than honest and friendly discussion for healthy confrontation or criticism. Whenever such unhealthy confrontations emerge, it is best, if at all possible, to simply walk away from the fight.

Having said this, I am a realist that understands sometimes your opponent doesn't share the same view and will leave you with the choice to surrender or stand and fight, without the option to simply walk away. Some things are worth fighting for; others demand a surrender. We must be able to see the difference and discern the best way to end a fight (evade, surrender, or conquer).

The Apostle Paul put it eloquently. "If possible, so far as it depends on you, live peaceably with all."[12] As he states, so long as it is possible, as much as it is in our control to do so, we must live at peace with one another. This doesn't mean we never have any healthy confrontations. Paul was well known for being the confrontational coach that was never afraid to challenge a wrong. It does mean that we avoid the unhealthy confrontations, to the best of our abilities.

In the first hypothetical situation, a mugger confronts me and asks for my wallet and any valuables I have on me. The value of these material possessions pales in comparison to the value of my life, or the lives of others around me (including the mugger's life), especially when considering I don't keep much cash in my wallet and credit cards are easily canceled. My tanden would supply very little motivation to attack but significant motivation to survive. In this situation, I would likely submit my possessions to this mugger to avoid a potentially life-threatening physical confrontation. There may be an exception if there was reason to believe that surrendering wouldn't result in the desired surviving of the situation or would likely result in a future encounter that threatened the life of either myself or another, but most likely I would surrender because the risk of failure in the confrontation outweighs the potential reward of success. Winning this fight is best accomplished by surrendering the low-value possessions. This allows me to survive to report the crime and let the police do their job to track down the mugger and bring him to justice.

In the second hypothetical situation, I'm confronted with a mugger who asks me to surrender my child. In this scenario, my tanden would instantly fill me with extreme passion and tenacity. My instinctive fatherly protector mode would explode right through that attacker and tear him apart. This explosion is not sourced from physical strength. Trust me: I'm not setting any global standards as a strongman. Instead, it is sourced purely from an attitude and will to win that believes failure is not an option. That mugger is not going to touch my child!

Performance

This relates to the action portion of our STAR model in that it represents the courage to take action, the drive that fuels the perspiration that comes with hard work, and the persistence to stick with it despite obstacles. And this all feeds from our strategy in that it requires a purpose we can believe in and a vision that inspires passion.

In the hypothetical situations, my vision includes the objective of safely rearing my children to become adults who contribute positively to society. In the first situation, there is no immediate threat to my child, and the best way to meet my objective is to take the steps necessary to ensure that I return home safely. If putting up a fight was the best way to ensure that objective, then I would put up a fight, but most likely surrendering my wallet would be the best option.

In the second situation, the mugger presents a major obstacle to my objective, and a direct threat to my child. This is an obstacle that I simply will not allow to interfere with progress. That is the attitude of tenacity that we must develop within ourselves for every objective in our plan. If we can't muster up that kind of never-quit tenacity, then we aren't likely to achieve the objective. And we must always remember that there is usually more than one way to achieve our objective. Weigh the cost, the risk, and the reward for your approach. Use wise judgment to discern the best option for the greatest probability of success. When you fail—and, at times, you will fail—get up and get back in the game. Don't let your failure keep you down. The well-known executive coach and author of multiple best sellers on leadership, John C. Maxwell, notes, "People who succeed develop an attitude of tenacity. They refuse to quit, and they are determined not to let failure defeat them."[13]

We have to possess that intense drive and motivation to succeed. This doesn't mean that we'll never fail. It does mean that we will view every failure as an opportunity to learn and a stepping-stone to success. In reality, we're likely to experience more failure than success. It has been said that "great people are not free from trouble [failure] they just deal with it differently than the masses."[14] Again, John C. Maxwell states that "the people who don't make mistakes end up working for those who do."[15]

> We have to possess that intense drive and motivation to succeed. This doesn't mean that we'll never fail. It does mean that we will view every failure as an opportunity to learn and a stepping-stone to success.

If the action we take is to produce the results we desire, we must practice diligently to keep our skills up so that we may perform optimally yet have the courage to take risks that will inevitably result in some failures along the way to success. We must work hard—never back away from an opportunity to perspire. We must persist and persevere in the face of adversity. To do all of this, we must have a strong attitude and tenacious desire to succeed. That is tanden.

Riki

The term *riki* means strength, power, proficiency, or ability. It can also be added as a suffix to a noun to provide the meaning of "the strength of [the noun]."[16] To the karateka, riki means physical power, strength of character and self-discipline, and proficiency of skill all applied in achievement both inside the dojo and out in the world.

The kata and prearrange motions in karate are designed for constant repetition that strengthens the body, increases flexibility, and trains the mind. The sensei will provide constant coaching and corrections meant to polish the karateka's skill and improve performance over time. As the student improves, the critical nature of the corrections will increase because the sensei knows that the student's understanding of the critique has increased.

Self-discipline is developed as the student endures the challenges of studying and learns not to quit. As the sensei coaches, "Get lower," the student knows to lower his/her center of gravity, which strains the leg muscles. The temptation is to rise in relief of this strain, but doing so will cheat the student of the strengthening to be gained. As the sensei offers correction, the student adjusts and applies what is learned. The goal is to improve a little each time.

Our character begins when our principles are defined and is strengthened (or weakened) as opportunities to give in, or break our principles, are faced. Each and every time we hold fast to our principles, our character is strengthened. Similarly, every time we give in to the temptation to sacrifice our principles, we weaken our character. In all of history, there has only been one perfect man that never sacrificed his principles. So don't beat yourself up over every infraction. But do learn from these failures and allow them to strengthen your resolve to hold fast to your principles in the future. It isn't about being perfect. It is about being strong, recognizing failure, and taking appropriate corrective action (including making apologies if appropriate).

To the *STAR Performer*, results are about the powerful delivery of solid action toward a sound plan. These results require strength of character, proficiency of skill, powerful follow through, self-discipline, introspection, and external monitoring and coaching. When applied together, these traits will lead to continually improving results. This is riki.

STAR

The order with which these precepts are applied is critical. "In karate practice we utilize the precepts in order of importance to form the moves of a kata. This materializes by first employing the eyes, then stepping out seeking proper balance, followed by a strong commitment and attitude and then the application of our strength to form and execute the movement with unbroken fluidity."[17]

The same is true for the philosophy of *STAR Performance*. Our success depends on proper sequencing in which we begin with employing the proverbial eyes with a solid **strategy** that defines purpose, declares principles, and inspires passion. This must be done first in order to know why you, or your organization, exist to begin with, what long-term objectives you will work toward, and what guiding principles will govern how you proceed. Taking any action or making any plans before defining these basics is like a tree with shallow, weak roots.

Next we can step out with proper balance, having a well-defined and well-thought-out tactical plan that includes proper preparation, planning, and prioritization. The **tactical** plan builds on the strategic foundation providing a bridge from the dream to a limitless, flourishing reality.

With this plan firmly in place, we express strong commitment and attitude through **action** that includes practice, persistence, and lots of good old-fashioned perspiration. As action is implemented, we maintain patience for optimal timing, strive for the most efficient productivity, and continually monitor to identify opportunities for improvement. Only then will we achieve the desired **results**.

This is the path to STAR Performance. This is how to generate successful results and create perfect performance. Great plans (strategy + tactics) followed up with energized doing (action + results) radiate increasingly enhanced performance—STAR Performance!

Attitudes

If we are to perform optimally, we must have the right attitude. We cannot think that time spent developing a strategy is time

Performance

wasted, and we also can't get bogged down in perpetual strategizing that never results in real action. We don't want to trudge forward without a plan, and we don't want to sit still forever without ever moving forward at all. We must not fear a challenge or be so afraid of failure that we never take a risk. We must be both strong and agile so that we have the ability to charge the obstacles and the agility to make rapid course corrections when needed.

> Before we can truly be honest with others, we must be honest with ourselves. Honesty with ourselves requires courage and a willingness to face our failures and learn from them.

We must never be afraid to admit failure or to identify areas that need improvement. Instead we must be quick with introspection and welcome honest criticism that opens our eyes to a better way of doing things. Honesty is more inward than outward. Before we can truly be honest with others, we must be honest with ourselves. Honesty with ourselves requires courage and a willingness to face our failures and learn from them.

Maintain optimism; avoid giving in to discouragement. Embrace change, because it is inevitable. If you are not the change agent, you will be the change victim. View problems as solutions in the making, and face them head on. Never hide them or pretend that they don't exist, for this will only make matters worse. Face your fears. In his first inauguration, Franklin D. Roosevelt stated "… let me assert my firm belief that the only thing we have to fear is … fear itself."[18] Don't let fear paralyze you.

Agility

Agility is the ability to think and act quickly. It involves the nimbleness to draw conclusions about what is going on around you and act based on those conclusions to adjust your plans.

There is an implication of flexibility, meaning that you are able to make appropriate course corrections to improve performance, adjust your target to changing conditions, or realign efforts to new priorities.

Demonstrating a high level of performance requires agility because, as the old adage states, the only thing in life that is constant is change. Market conditions will change. Products will become obsolete. Competitors will improve on your offering. Prices will rise and fall. Opportunities will come and go. Team members will come and go. Some people will come to your aid, and others will betray you. One year your profit will excel, and another you will scrape by. Today a hurricane is beating at your door, but the forecast for tomorrow is clear, blue skies. Change is inevitable.

As I'm writing this, I'm reminded of the process through which rockets are launched into space. I live in Central Florida—close enough to Kennedy Space Center to watch launches from my backyard. The local news will announce expected launches, and most everyone that lives locally knows and understands that there are often delays in the launch plans. Something freezes, a sensor gives a stray reading, a pump isn't working, the weather won't cooperate, or (my personal favorite) a "tourist" strayed too close in his boat.

There are so many things that can cause a launch delay; it is a wonder that any rocket ever launches. Yet they do. They do because the launch teams are agile. They plan carefully, including contingency plans. There is a checklist for every possible scenario meant to assure that they don't launch until ready, and when they do launch, the mission is successful. They are able to adapt to changing conditions—weather, equipment malfunction, onlookers in the wrong place, or whatever problem arises. To be clear, there have been some major failures; even a few that resulted in loss of life. But have you stopped to think about the fact that they are literally lifting people and/or cargo right off the face of the earth and into space yet have a tremendously high success rate? I don't know the exact percentage of successful space launches, but I'm certain it is very, very high.

Consider these statistics for NASA's Space Shuttle Program:

- 98.5 percent mission success rate—that's 1.5 percent mission critical failure rate (two missions out of 135 that ended in critical failure).
- In 135 missions, the shuttle lifted 3.5 million pounds of cargo into space and returned 229,132 pounds to earth.
- The shuttles made approximately 21,000 orbits and spent 1,323 days in space.
- There were a total of 833 individual crewmembers (some flying multiple missions), and fourteen of these crewmembers sacrificed their lives during the two critical mission failures.[19]

I don't want to downplay the significance of these failures. The loss of life is heartbreaking and humbling. My point is only that the major catastrophe is quite rare. It makes the evening news in a dramatic way when it does happen, but the vast majority of launches go off without a hitch. And this is despite the fact that it is basically a really large dart fitted with tons of high-intensity explosives intended to lift an incredible amount of weight to unbelievable heights.

This is the kind of agility we need to demonstrate in order to constantly improve. We do not want to be easily blown about by every little breeze of a challenge but to have a steadfast focus on our goals and objectives that allows us to make intelligent decisions and coarse corrections that increase our probability of success. The running back that drives straight into a defender doesn't usually get too far. But the running back that makes a quick course change based on the position and formation of the defense, and waits on his blocker to hold the defender back, is far more likely to pick up yardage on the play. For the running back, speed and strength are very important, but agility is critical. The same is true for you and me as we make our way through our life journeys. Improvement in our performance requires agility in our actions and plans.

Introspection

Our ability to be introspective is critical as well. Without introspection, it is impossible to demonstrate intelligent agility. We can't be afraid to ask the tough questions. We can't hide from the truth. We won't be able to improve if we aren't willing to admit a deficiency and propose a solution. Admitting a failure is the first step in turning a failure into a success, while hiding a failure is the first step in jumping off a cliff. John C. Maxwell states, "Successful people understand the role failure plays in achievement. ... the milestones on the road of success are always failures."[20]

If we lack the willingness or ability to look within and ask the tough questions, then we lack the ability to improve performance. Making improvements requires both the agility to adjust to changing conditions around us and the character to see truth in the mirror so that flaws or weaknesses can be improved. You can't fix something that you don't know is wrong, and you'll never correct it if you can't admit it needs to be corrected.

Honesty begins with an inward look. It we can't be honest with ourselves, we won't be honest with others. Somehow we have developed the notion that making a mistake is a horrible thing. That somehow our character is lessened when we fail or commit an error. I would assert that just the opposite is true. If we truly never fail at anything, it can only be because we aren't taking risks or stretching ourselves to do better.

Don't be afraid of risk. Don't be afraid of mistakes or failures. And most importantly, don't be too proud to admit mistakes and failures. A failure won't destroy you, but pride will. There is an ancient Hebrew proverb that teaches, "Pride goes before destruction, and a haughty spirit before a fall" (Proverbs 16:18 ESV).[21] In other words, if we are too proud to learn from our mistakes, then we will be doomed to repeat them to the point of destruction. Pride keeps you from seeing the failure as a milestone along the path to success. Pride causes you to pretend that the failure never happened and dooms you to live with the failure forever. Pride will destroy your efforts to excel and improve and may even cause you, your team, or your organization to crash and burn.

> Don't be afraid of risk. Don't be afraid of mistakes or failures. And most importantly, don't be too proud to admit mistakes and failures. A failure won't destroy you, but pride will.

The only fatal mistakes in life are those that we try to hide or pretend never happened. These are the mistakes that we don't learn any lessons from. These are the failures we are doomed to repeat. In fact, if we do learn a little something from every mistake and failure, then we get better and better with every mistake we make. So mistakes are actually a good thing. They are fantastic teachers. Successes make us feel good and of course are the objective of all the hard work. But failures teach us the lessons we must learn if we are to repeat the success in a manner beyond reliance on blind luck. Again gleaning insight from the masterful teacher, John C. Maxwell, we see that "a man must be big enough to admit his mistakes, smart enough to profit from them, and strong enough to correct them."[22]

At the end of the day, we have three choices for how we respond to our failures: allow our pride to dominate us such that we hide or ignore our mistakes, allow our mistakes to dominate us such that we cower in fear of further failure, or learn from our mistakes and embrace the opportunity to improve. I choose the third option. What about you?

Improvement

The chapter on "Results" is all about making improvements. I won't waste your time by repeating everything covered there but will simply offer a brief summary to help drill it in.

Improvement is key. We need to be continually improving our efforts, our processes, our team, and our execution. This applies to everything about what we do and how we do it. To make this happen, we have to start with clear goals and objectives, follow this with tangible action that is continually monitored and measured, and make course corrections along the way to optimize our journey.

We also have to work together well as a team. This means if there are people on the team that are divisive or detrimental to the team as a whole, they must be removed quickly. There have been athletes that had tremendous individual talent but lacked a team spirit and desire to make those around them excel. These individuals struggle to perform at their peak because they view themselves as superior and don't work well with others. If you can coach this person to see the value in self-sacrifice and team involvement, rather than self-promotion and grandstanding, you will capitalize on a potential for greatness that is contagious and spreads throughout your team. If, on the other hand, this person's pride keeps them from accepting such coaching, then they simply must be removed as quickly as possible, because keeping them in place will tear down the entire team. This leads into the need for mentors in every performance enhancing organization.

I'd also like to discuss a tool that I've found helpful in managing our introspection and identifying areas in need of improvement. This tool was introduced in my first book, *Centurion Living: Life Planning Fundamentals*, in which it was applied to your personal life plan. I described a wheel of "mission fields" such that each mission field provides the spoke of a wheel—a "wheel of life." The mission fields are simply areas of our lives in which we live out our purpose and have missions and objectives.[23]

Each of the "spokes" in this wheel are inflated independently. If every one of our mission fields is operating perfectly, our "wheel of life" is perfectly round—all spokes are inflated equally. However, when areas begin to lag behind perfection, we have underinflated spokes and the wheel is no longer round. This easily provides the imagery of a very bumpy and uneven ride. It's worse than an underinflated tire on your car; it's a very uneven, bouncy ride that will rattle you to death if you don't take corrective action.

Worse yet is the prospect of having a "wheel of life" that is uncentered. This is what happens when we lack a clear sense of purpose. We can think of the center of the wheel, the axle, as being our core purpose. The different areas in our life become focused in different directions when we don't have a universal purpose to keep them centered. The result is a total breakdown of the wheel. It becomes a chaotic mess of disjointed spokes. When this happens, our lives will feel out of focus, overwhelming, and totally out of commission. While an underinflated section, or sections, will result in a bumpy ride, a "wheel" without a center just won't roll.

STAR Performance

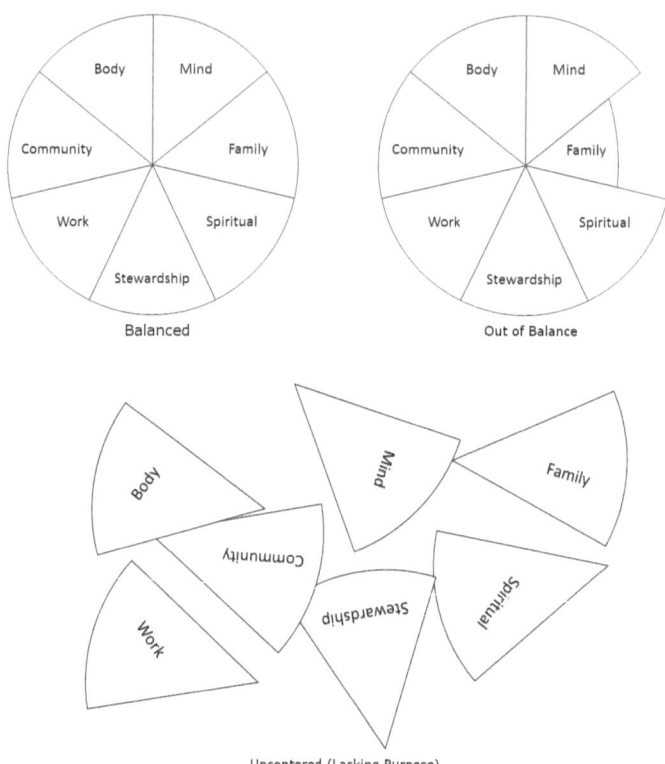

This same "wheel of life" concept can be applied to our businesses. In fact, it can be applied at both the strategic level (missions and objectives) and the tactical level (programs and goals).

Let's consider the strategic level application first. Your objectives may be broken down into categories, such as financial (margin growth), sales (revenue growth), organizational (team building, employee engagement, etc.), operational (process efficiencies, best-practices application, etc.), market (customer satisfaction, market penetration, etc.), culture (the build and sustainment of the desire culture within the organization), and community (how the company gives back to the community both corporately and individually). This is a generic categorization of objectives. Yours may look different; that's okay. The point is that our "strategy wheel" is built with spokes that are our objectives, or categories of objectives.

Performance

Balanced Strategy Wheel   Unbalanced Strategy Wheel

As we proceed with our plan, we can periodically review how we are doing. I typically recommend a quarterly review of our strategy wheel. As we are in the assessment process, we take a look at each spoke in the wheel—each objective, or category of objectives—and grade it on a scale of 0 to 100 percent.* If everything if perfectly on schedule and there are no unforeseen challenges pending to a given objective, then it would be scored a perfect 100 percent. If, on the other hand, our efforts toward that objective were completely stalled and falling apart, we would rate it a low 10 percent. Once we've graded each spoke of our strategy wheel, we can adjust its size accordingly. A grade of 100 would be full size, a grade of 50 would be half size, and a 10 would be very small. This creates an instant image of what our actual strategy wheel looks like. It is easy to visualize how round (or out of round) it actually is.

---

* You may select the granularity of metric measurement that is most appropriate for your organization. Typically, I would suggest a 10 percent scale (10 percent, 20 percent, 30 percent ... 100 percent), but you may choose to measure to a 5 percent, or even down to 1 percent, if that is more helpful in your case.

| 107 |

In the example graphic shown, the sales, marketing, and community objectives seem to be doing relatively well while the operational and financial objectives are lagging behind. In all likelihood, this is because the organization and culture just aren't what they need to be, as indicated by the very small spokes. Further digging is needed to understand what is actually going on, but the instant visualization will help steer you in the right direction for root-cause analysis and subsequent corrective actions. If you never do this assessment, then you will likely not even know that corrective action was needed until it is too late.

Identifying the metrics by which these assessments are measured is critical. Objectives should be measurable, so simply dividing the objective value by the number of assessment periods should provide a good estimate of where progress should be at any specific assessment time. In some cases, it may not be this simple because progress will not be linear across the period. Often an educated best guess will suffice in these cases.

We can apply the exact same exercise at the tactical level. In this case, each spoke in the wheel represents a particular program in our tactical plan. The spokes may be something like the following:

- development of widget X
- cost reduction initiative
- business process improvement initiative
- marketing campaign
- restructuring
- market Y penetration

The goals within the program make the assessment simple. If you're on schedule, and anticipate staying on schedule, the score will be high. If you are behind schedule and do not envision getting back on schedule anytime soon, the score will be low.

With this tool, you can quickly visualize where you stand at any given assessment. If you are on track and well balanced, you'll have a nearly perfect wheel that keeps you moving. If any of the spokes are falling behind, the need for decisive corrective action will be obvious.

Mentor

You need to fill your team with strong mentors. To do this, you must first be a strong mentor. A mentor can be a micromanager at times, when the mentee is new to a particular task and needs heavy guidance. However, a mentor never desires to micromanage any task. Instead, the mentor's goal is to transfer the skill and ability to perform to the mentee. Once the mentee develops enough skill to take over the execution of the task, the mentor needs to step back and let the mentee run with it—even if it results in mistakes or you know you could complete it faster. If you always step in and do it yourself, the mentee will never learn. Both of you will suffer as a result.

I think of my relationship with my children. Although I would never suggest comparing your team to children, or treating them like children, the parent-child relationship is a tremendous example of mentor-mentee interaction. I often involve my children in tasks that I could complete much more easily if I just did them myself. One of them will want to help me with a particular task—maybe it is assembling something, repairing something, or cleaning something. Most of the time, I can do these tasks rather quickly and very efficiently if I just do them myself.

Involving my children will often cause the task to take two to three times as long to complete and introduce a very high probability of some level of failure that likely requires me to come back later and repeat the task (undoing what was done so that it can be done correctly). I have a number of pieces of prefab furniture in our home that have stripped screws, missing joints, scratched surfaces, or other blemishes because I had the help of my children in putting them together. That's the down side to involving them in the process.*

The advantage to involving my children is that they now know how to use a hammer, screwdriver, cordless drill, and touch-up pen. They still have a lot of room to improve in these skills, which is why they'll be involved in the next assembly project as well. If I did all of this myself and never let them help, the work would have been done faster, with fewer errors (hopefully), but I would remain the only one in the house that knows how to do these things. That's not fair to me—or to my children.

Being a good mentor requires showing first and then allowing the mentee to make their own mistakes. A good mentee doesn't interrupt the process to avoid the mistake, unless, of course, the mistake would cause catastrophic harm. I'll let my children create a blemish on the furniture they help me assemble, but I will step in immediately to stop unsafe conduct that might result in the loss of a finger, or worse. Instead, the mentor guides the mentee to see how the mistake was made, how to correct it, and how to avoid it in the future. When my kids strip a screw, bend a nail, or scratch the furniture, rather than panic about it I will talk it through with them until they understand what went wrong, and why—so they have the ability to avoid the same mistake next time.

In these cases, I am micromanaging their work, but note that micromanaging is not the same thing as pushing them aside and doing it myself because I know that I can do it better. Instead, good micromanagement is letting them do the work while I monitor the effort closely, act as a coach to guide their thought

---

* Truthfully, all of the blemishes that result from getting the inexperienced help of my children are things that I consider marks of love that I will look back on with great affection and nostalgia when they are grown. Perhaps we should have a similar perspective of care and concern for those that we lead in our organizations.

processes, and intervene when they get off track to guide them back to task. It isn't about a lack of trust. It is about a proactive transfer of skill. In this way, micromanagement is a mentoring tool used to guide the mentee in learning so that your level of oversight can gradually decrease over time, until you are able to delegate and trust that it will be done effectively and efficiently without your supervision at all.

Not only must you be a good mentor to your team, but you also must develop a culture of mentorship in which your team members are eager to mentor one another. Some teams have a culture of secrecy around how individuals perform their tasks. There seems to be a philosophy of territorial protection as if "my job is more secure if no one else knows how to do it like I do." You cannot allow this culture to prevail. Instead, a culture of teamwork, cross-training, and workload sharing is imperative. If any task you might face can be handled by multiple people on your team, then team members will be able to help one another when a task falls behind schedule. You'll avoid the situation where tasks go undone because someone was out sick, on vacation, disappeared after winning the lottery, or—heaven forbid—died suddenly.

The only way that this can happen is if your team has a culture of mentoring that drives team members to enjoy sharing their skills and abilities with one another. This culture starts with you. Set the pace and be the example. Seek out people you can mentor, and seek out mentors that are willing and able to help you grow.

This is the path to STAR Performance. This is how to generate successful results and create perfect performance. Great plans (strategy + tactics) followed up with energized doing (action + results) radiate increasingly enhanced performance—STAR Performance!

STAR Performance

Strategy	
Purpose	why we exist
Principle	values we live by
Passion	inspiring vision built on mission and objectives

Tactics	
Prepare	getting ready
Plan	defining how, with goals and milestones
Prioritize	putting things in proper order

Action	
Practice	rehearsing and doing
Persistence	showing up
Perspiration	hard work

Results	
Patience	realistic expectations
Productivity	execution
Probing	introspection

Review

1. What does *performance* imply?

2. What are we talking about when we say *performance*?

3. What is the connection between performance and the STAR methodology?

4. What are the precepts of gan, soku, tanden, and riki? How do they relate to the STAR methodology?

5. Is the order in which the precepts of the STAR methodology are applied important? Why, or why not?

6. What is a *mission field*?

7. What happens when our *wheel of life* or *wheel of strategy* is unbalanced?

8. What happens when these wheels are uncentered (e.g., not targeting common purpose or mission)?

9. Who are your mentors (living and/or historical)?

10. Who can/should you be mentoring? What are you going to do about it?

11. Describe a list of objectives for each of the mission fields in your wheel of life (updated wheel provided in worksheet 8).

   physical

   intellectual

   spiritual

   family

   friends

   stewardship

   work

   community

Use worksheet 8 in the appendix for routine follow-up to grade how you are doing and visualize how balanced your wheel is at that moment.

12. Describe a list of objectives for each of the mission fields in your organizations wheel of strategy. (Change the general mission fields listed to suit your organization if necessary.)

culture

financial

sales

market

organization

operations

products/services

community

Use worksheet 9 in the appendix for routine follow-up to grade how you are doing and visualize how balanced your wheel is at that moment.

Notes

1. Scaglione, Robert and William Cummins. *Karate of Okinawa: Building a Warrior Spirit with Gan, Soku, Tanden, Riki*. Person-to-Person Publishing. New York. 1989.
2. "Dojo Rules." *Basics*. Shorin-Ryu Karate USA. Web. February 24, 2015. <http://www.suntreekarate.com/Basics.html>.
3. Funakoshi, Gichin and Genwa Nakasone (translated by John Teramoto). *The Twenty Guiding Principles of Karate*. Kodansha USA, 2012.
4. Ibid, 19–20.
5. Nagamine, Shoshin. *The Essence of Okinawan Karate-Do*. Tuttle, 1976, 48.
6. Scaglione, Robert and William Cummins. *Karate of Okinawa: Building a Warrior Spirit with Gan, Soku, Tanden, Riki*. Person-to-Person Publishing. New York, 1989, 33.
7. "Kanji for Soku | Free Kanji Translation." *Kanji for Soku*. JP41. Web. February 24, 2015. <http://www.jp41.com/kanji/soku.html>.
8. Instructions routinely provided by Hanshi Scaglione in lessons. He reiterates that he is providing the same instructions that his Hanshi, Master Ansei Ushero, provided for decades.
9. George, Patrick. "How Aerodynamics Works, Aerodynamic Add-ons." HowStuffWorks. Web. February 24, 2015.
10. Bonsor, Kevin and Karim Nice. "NASCAR Restraint System—HowStuffWorks." *HowStuffWorks*. InfoSpace. Web. February 24, 2015.
11. Scaglione, Robert and William Cummins. *Karate of Okinawa: Building a Warrior Spirit with Gan, Soku, Tanden, Riki*. Person-to-Person Publishing. New York. 1989, 63.
12. "Romans 12:18." The Holy Bible: English Standard Version. Crossway Bibles. 2001.
13. Maxwell, John C. *The Difference Maker: Making Your Attitude Your Greatest Asset*. Nelson. 2006, 153.
14. Scaglione, Robert and William Cummins. *Karate of Okinawa: Building a Warrior Spirit with Gan, Soku, Tanden, Riki*. Person-to-Person Publishing. New York, 1989, 77.
15. Maxwell, John C. *The Difference Maker: Making Your Attitude Your Greatest Asset*. Nelson. 2006, 151.
16. "Riki." *Jeffrey's Japanese/English Dictionary*. Web. February 25, 2015.
17. Scaglione, Robert and William Cummins. *Karate of Okinawa: Building a Warrior Spirit with Gan, Soku, Tanden, Riki*. Person-to-Person Publishing. New York. 1989, 99.

[18] "'Only Thing We Have to Fear Is Fear Itself': FDR's First Inaugural Address." *History Matters*. American Social History Production, George Mason University. Web. April 9, 2015. <http://historymatters.gmu.edu/d/5057/>.

[19] Malik, Tariq. "NASA's Space Shuttle by the Numbers: 30 Years of a Spaceflight Icon." Space.com. Purch, July 21, 2011. Web. July 9, 2015.

[20] Ibid, 160.

[21] "Proverbs 16:18." The Holy Bible: English Standard Version. Crossway Bibles. 2001.

[22] Maxwell, John C. *The Power of Leadership*. David C. Cook. January 20, 2015, 2001.

[23] Thompson, Justin. *Centurion Living: Life Planning Fundamentals*. WestBow Press. 2012, 181.

Appendix—Worksheets

The worksheets in the following pages are meant to be guides for your discussion and planning activities. You may use them as presented or use them for inspiration to create your own worksheets. Good luck!

1. Defining Your Purpose
2. Defining Principles
3. Defining Mission
4. Defining Objectives
5. Strategy Development Worksheet
6. Tactics Planning 1
7. Tactics Planning 2
8. Life Wheel Checkup
9. Strategy Wheel Checkup
10. Blank Wheel Checkup

Worksheet 1: Defining Your Purpose

Consider each of the following discussion questions and review with your team. Keep going through these and asking, "Why?" until you converge on the most fundamental reason for existing. You may add questions or adjust as needed for your specific needs.

List the three most fundamental reasons for existence.

1._____

2._____

3._____

Of these three, which is most fundamental?

Ask yourself, and your team, "Why are these reasons for existence important?"

Will any of these reasons for existing ever change?

Are any of these reasons for existing actually missions or objectives?

Worksheet 2: Defining Principles

List five important guiding principles that you consider nonnegotiable. (You may use multiple worksheets if you have more than five to list.)

1. _____

2. _____

3. _____

4. _____

5. _____

In the space provided below, describe why each principle is important and why it is nonnegotiable.

Worksheet 3: Defining Mission

Use this worksheet to help guide your discussion on defining your strategic mission. Larger organizations may have multiple missions; just keep in mind that you have limited resources. Don't take on more mission than your resources can handle.

What do you believe is your core mission?

How does this mission fulfill, or align with, your purpose? Or does it?

What adjustments need to be made to your mission to bring it into alignment with purpose?

What are the five most important indicators of fulfillment of this mission?

1. _____
2. _____
3. _____
4. _____
5. _____

Worksheet 4: Defining Objectives

What are the three most important things for you to accomplish in the next twelve months?

1._____
2._____
3._____

Are the above items strategic or tactical?

1._____
2._____
3._____

Are any of the strategic items listed above elements of a common objective, or are they discrete objectives?

Reword the remaining discrete strategic objectives for clarity. (Come back to the nonstrategic items later. They may be tactical goals.)

These are your one-year objectives.

Do your one-year objectives align with your mission? Do they overlap with your five most important indicators of mission fulfillment?

If not, make adjustments to mission and/or objectives until they do.

Repeat this worksheet for three-year objectives and five-year objectives.

Worksheet 5: Strategy Development

Your Purpose

What fundamental purpose did your discussion from worksheet 1 reveal?

Your Mission

What is the "big picture" of what you intend to accomplish? (This should have come out of worksheet 3 discussion.)

Your Objectives

Define clear, distinct, and measureable outcomes to be fulfilled in your desired future. (This should have resulted from worksheet 4.)

1.

2.

3.

4.

5.

Your Vision Statement

Combine your purpose and mission, with objectives added in for clarity as needed, into a single phrase or short paragraph that communicates them in an inspiring way.

Worksheet 6: Tactics Planning 1

Defining Operations/Programs

Applicable Objective

Simply restate the objective(s) that this plan applies to. Repeat the worksheet for each objective.

Key Areas of Focus

Define each of the key areas of focus that need a plan in order to reach the objective(s).

-
-
-
-
-

Your Program/Operations

List the specific programs or operations that will be embarked upon to address each area of focus. Give each program or operation a name.

1.

2.

3.

4.

5.

Worksheet 7: Tactics Planning 2

Planning Operations/Programs

Operation _____

List the applicable program or operation (e.g., operation team builder or operation new markets). Provide a clarifying statement defining the operation for the specific program or operation.

Goals

Define the key goals of the operation. Use multiple sheets if necessary.

1. Responsible:_____
   Due date:_____
   Description:

2. Responsible:_____
   Due date:_____
   Description:

3. Responsible:_____
   Due date:_____
   Description:

4. Responsible:_____
   Due date:_____
   Description:

5. Responsible:_____
   Due date:_____
   Description:

Worksheet 8: Life Wheel Checkup

Each spoke is graduated with lines representing 10 percent segments. Rate each mission field (spoke) as 10 percent, 20 percent, 30 percent ... 100 percent, and shade in the appropriate number of segments to visualize how well balanced your life is at this moment.

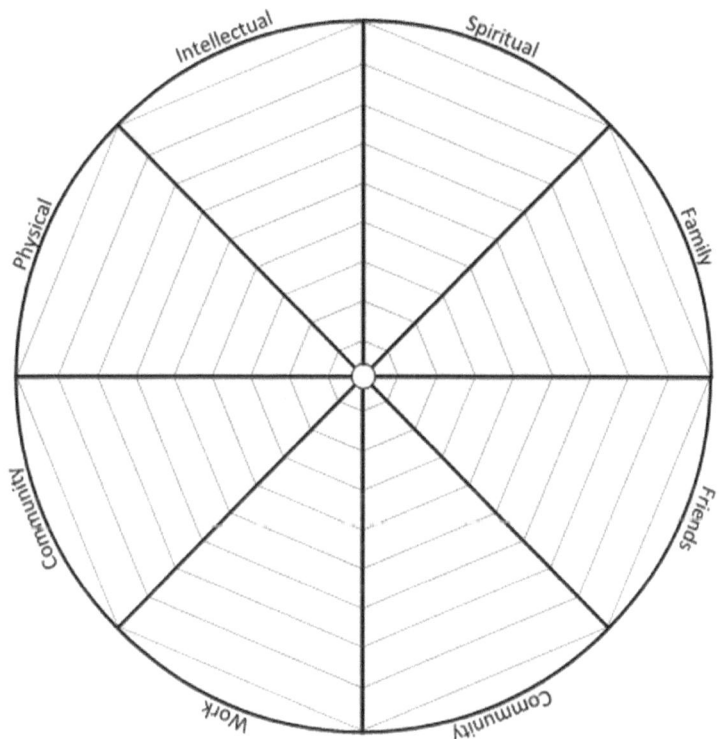

Worksheet 9: Strategy Wheel Checkup

Each spoke is graduated with lines representing 10 percent segments. Rate each mission field (spoke) as 10 percent, 20 percent, 30 percent … 100 percent, and shade in the appropriate number of segments to visualize how well balanced your life is at this moment.

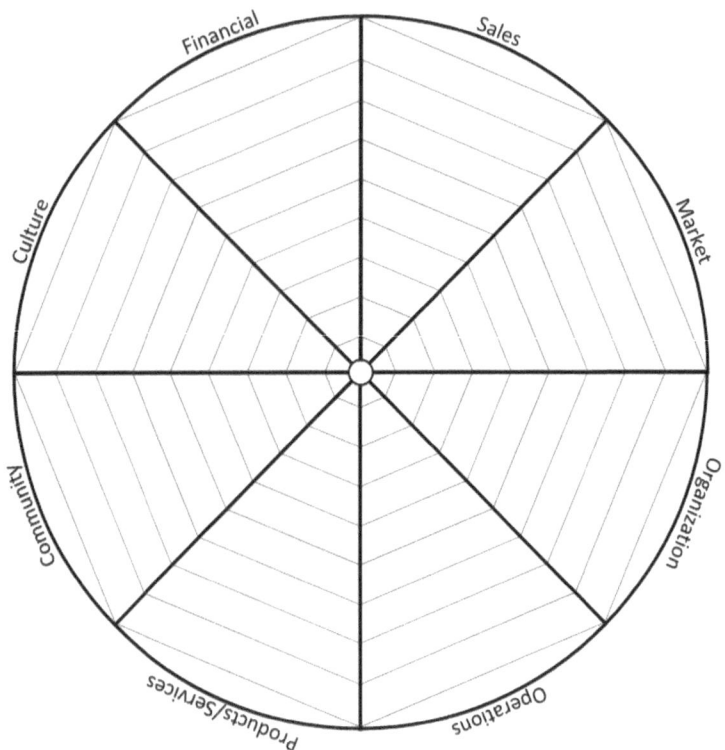

Worksheet 10: Blank Wheel Checkup

Each spoke is graduated with lines representing 10 percent segments. First, define each mission field (spoke in the wheel). Next, rate each mission field as 10 percent, 20 percent, 30 percent ... 100 percent, and shade in the appropriate number of segments to visualize how well balanced your life is at this moment.

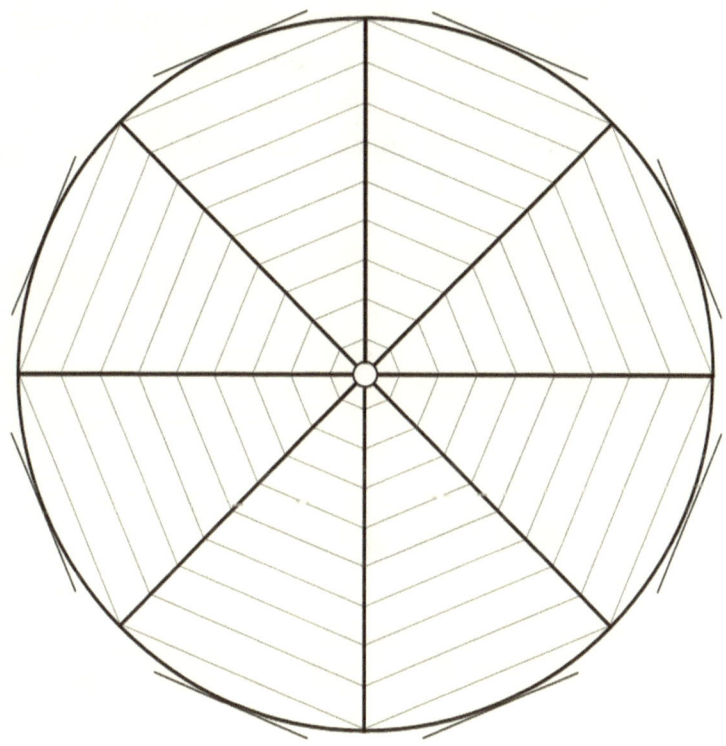

Acknowledgement

I would like to offer a special thanks to my wife, Tanya, for encouraging me to take the steps necessary to step out on my own, to serve by sharing insights, and to complete this book. Thanks also go to my children, Joshua and Hannah, for their unconditional love and inspiration, and to my parents, Mike and Lynn, for teaching me the value of self-sacrifice and self-discipline. Thanks, Grandmother Joyce, for setting an example for strength, resilience, and can-do attitude through a multitude of joys and sorrows over nearly a century of positive living. And, most importantly, I thank my Lord and Savior Jesus Christ for sacrificial love and being the greatest leader of all time!

About the Author

Dr. Justin Thompson is a visionary leader with a passion for intentional team building and mentoring. His desire is to influence people to be confident individuals who are harmonious parts of a thriving team or organization. He is the founder and CEO of 2Xalt, Inc., an organization created with the purpose to exalt the performance of individuals, teams, and organizations. He has developed the STAR model for personal and organizational excellence. As described in this book, this model unites planning with doing.

Dr. Thompson has nearly two decades of experience in technology businesses, holding roles of increasing responsibility from the manufacturing floor to the C suite. In every role, regardless of org-chart hierarchy, Justin has enjoyed the impact of inspiring others and helping them to imagine the possibilities of what they could accomplish if they work with unity of purpose toward common goals and objectives.

LinkedIn: linkedin.com/in/thompsonj1

Facebook: www.facebook.com/2Xalt

Google+:   plus.google.com/+JustinThompson2Xalt

Twitter: @2XaltU

Additional Rescources

Centurion Living: Life Planning Fundamentals

Discover the meaning of life. What is your core purpose? What values define your character, and why? What missions should fill your life, and how do you prioritize them?

This book was written to help you develop a strategic life plan. It builds on the simple story in Scripture about an unnamed man, a centurion in the Roman army, who sent for Jesus because his servant was ill and near death. Jesus responded to this man, who was not a Jew, by stating that He had not experienced such faith from anyone else in all of Israel. This simple story gives us a powerful life lesson and a solid example for us to follow in our lives.

www.CenturionVision.com

Centurion Living Study Guide

This workbook is designed as a guide to learn and apply the principles of purpose taught in *Centurion Living*. Its fill-in-the-blank style leaves room for your thoughts and notes as you study through the information. It can be studied individually, but you'll get the most out of it when studied in a group setting with open discussion.

www.CenturionVision.com

Centurion Living Leader's Guide

This leader's guide is a companion to the study guide that provides the answers to the fill-in-the-blank workbook and adds a few additional insights to help the leader guide small group interactions as they study and learn together.

www.CenturionVision.com

2Xalt STAR Programs and Services

2Xalt exists to encourage passion, to generate confidence, and to exalt (2Xalt) performance in individuals, teams, and organizations. We accomplish this by providing impactful executive coaching and expert consulting designed to help those we serve to plan effectively, execute efficiently, and improve continuously.

www.2Xalt.com

Leadership 2Xalt Performance

Institute 2Xalt Leadership

The Institute 2Xalt Leadership is an online school providing low cost training for today's businesses, organizations, and individuals (learn.2Xalt.com). New courses are constantly being developed to add to the training provided, with course covering the following topics either currently offered or in development:

★ Maintaining Life Balance
★ Maintaining Business Balance
★ Cultivating STAR Performance
★ Developing STAR Leadership
★ Creating a Business Plan
★ A Startup Checklist
★ Time Management

Scan this page and email to the course instructor to claim your free coaching session with a certified professional coach with purchase of the course.

 learn.2Xalt.com

Premier Executive Coaching

★ **2Xalt TRUST: Executive Peer Advisory Board**

Your 'brain-trust' for business. Discover new confidence and clarity with the guidance of your personal peer advisory council, facilitated by a certified executive coach.

★ **2Xalt 1-2-1: Personalized Executive Coaching**

Like a world class athlete, you'll create enhanced clarity and accomplishment with the guidance of a personal executive coach to lead you through the process of casting vision, setting goals, and monitoring progress.

★ **2Xalt TEAM: Team Executive Coaching**

Coaching will help your team achieve new levels of meaningful accomplishment by focusing on what's most important while avoiding unproductive distractions. You will see your team begin to function with harmonious unity of purpose and mission, and the powerful diversity of non-uniformity.

★ **2Xalt WORK: Customized Workshops**

For those in need of making an immediate impact on specific issues and opportunities, rather than ongoing coaching, we offer specialized workshops that generate awareness, create passion, and drive results.

2Xalt

Subject Matter Expert Consulting

★ **2Xalt ORG: ASSESSMENT & DEVELOPMENT**

Organization | Operations | Exec Team | Plans
Discover clarity. Build awareness. Create a meaningful path forward to thriving, productive organizations and operations.

★ **2Xalt LEADERSHIP: INTERIM & P/T EXECUTIVES**

Interim C-Suite Leaders | Director | Advisory Board
Fill a critical gap on your leadership team without a long-term commitment. Generate new insight and clarity by augmenting your board or executive team with our seasoned executives.

★ **2Xalt DISCERNMENT: Investor and Board Advising**

Strategy & Tactics Advising | M&A Due Diligence | Business Plan
Our expert consultants have the knowledge and skills to provide assessment and advisement that will enhance judgement, and create an abundance of high value discernment.

★ **2Xalt SME: SUBJECT MATTER EXPERT Services**

Product Mgt | Program Mgt | Surveillance | Technology | EO/IR | Systems Engineering | BD | Sales Process | MARCOM | Govt Contracting | General Mgt
Our professional services are designed 2xalt your operations when you need a short term boost. We provide subject matter experts for technical programs, and operational assessment and development services.

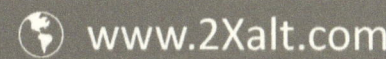

www.2Xalt.com

www.ingramcontent.com/pod-product-compliance
Lightning Source LLC
Chambersburg PA
CBHW030758180526
45163CB00003B/1079